M000235010
Enjoy Rome!!
Kay & Deke

Fleeting Rome

Fleeting Rome

In Search of La Dolce Vita

Carlo Levi

Translated by Tony Shugaar

John Wiley & Sons, Ltd

This edition published in 2004 by John Wiley & Sons, Ltd, The Atrium, Southern Gate
Chichester, West Sussex, PO19 8SQ, England
Phone (+44) 1243 779777

Original edition published in Italian by Donzelli Editore, Rome.

English language edition published by arrangement with Eulama Literary Agency, Rome, Italy.

E-mail (for orders and customer service enquires): cs-books@wiley.co.uk
Visit our Home Page on www.wiley.co.uk or www.wiley.com

Other Wiley Editorial Offices
John Wiley & Sons, Inc. 111 River Street, Hoboken, NJ 07030, USA

Jossey-Bass, 989 Market Street, San Francisco, CA 94103-1741, USA

Wiley-VCH Verlag GmbH, Pappellaee 3, D-69469 Weinheim, Germany

John Wiley & Sons Australia, Ltd, 33 Park Road, Milton, Queensland, 4064, Australia

John Wiley & Sons (Asia) Pte Ltd, 2 Clementi Loop #02-01, Jin Xing Distripark, Singapore 129809

John Wiley & Sons Canada Ltd, 22 Worcester Road, Etobicoke, Ontario, Canada, M9W 1L1

Wiley also publishes its books in a variety of electronic formats. Some content that appears in print may not be available in electronic books.

Library of Congress Cataloging-in-Publication Data
A catalog record for this book is available from the US Library of Congress

British Library Cataloguing in Publication Data
A catalogue record for this book is available from the British Library

ISBN 0-470-87183-0

Typeset in 9.5/14 pt Arrus by Sparks, Oxford – www.sparks.co.uk
Printed and bound in Great Britain by TJ International Ltd, Padstow, Cornwall

This book is printed on acid-free paper responsibly manufactured from sustainable forestry in which at least two trees are planted for each one used for paper production.

10 9 8 7 6 5 4 3 2 1

Contents

Preface

By Gigliola De Donato and Luisa Montevecchi

Carlo Levi's varied and prolific literary career (political, social and ethnological, artistic, and critical essays, travel writing and reporting), which ranged broadly over a wide array of subjects (from popular culture to news reporting, from personal and family reminiscences to topical observations on events, occurrences, personalities, and protagonists of history in the making), is for the most part preserved in his personal archive, the 'site'. We have relied upon this as the source of material in this volume, which has been selected from the mass of writings that Levi either chose not to organize or never had the time to organize.

A preliminary classification of Carlo Levi's papers has already been undertaken by his friend and partner in life, Linuccia Saba and, however pragmatic the criteria may have been, toward the end of the 1970s, the reorganization was by and large complete.

This initial organization arranged Carlo Levi's papers into four main sections: 1) correspondence; 2) documents; 3) photographic archive; 4) exhibition catalogues.

It is only now, however, following a period in which the collection of papers was entrusted to the skilled care of the *Archivio Centrale dello Stato* (Italy's Central State Archives) and thanks to the careful reorganization carried out by Doctor Margherita Martelli and Doctor Luisa Montevecchi under the supervision of the new director, Professor Paola Carucci, that the *Fondo Carlo Levi* (Carlo Levi Collection) is now fully available to those who are interested in pursuing a more complete understanding of the literary, civil, and artistic work of this author.

Making use of the reorganization carried out by the Central State Archives, we have selected various types of writing on that basis. All the same, they have been obliged to discriminate carefully, establishing distinctions within the categories, taking care to identify, among the varied interests of the Turin-born intellectual, often coexisting in a single essay, not only the specific 'subjects' of the various essays, but also the interference or interdependence of 'other' interests within a given subject matter. In other words, we did not limit ourselves to the general criterion of content, but also focused on the modality of the writing, the tone and the inflection.

Dividing the essays into sections may seem like a clinical, even surgical undertaking, but we were convinced that it was necessary to provide a structure to the multiform richness of Levi's world, the circularity of his ideas and images, often existing side-by-side in a rhapsodic navigation of memory or thought. We found that the only valid criteria would be ones whereby we could offer an image of the author in all the modulations of his singular keyboard. Only the reader can say if we have been successful. The 'Introduction' to the individual essays, and the 'Notes to the Text', may offer a useful guide in reading.

These criteria have led to the outline set forth in the "Plan of the Work". In reference to the classification of the essays, we should make a further distinction: while travel writing, essays in historical and political thought, essays on theory, and literary and art criticism are all objectively unified by the specific subject matter of each, the other essays, prompted by specific occasions, have been classified according to their internal thematic homogeneity (writings about Rome, writings about Italy, writings on reflections or recollections, writings inspired by the animal world).

All of these writings are now published in book form for the first time, but other 'unpublished' material can be found. Firstly the *Fondo Manoscritti di Autori Moderni e Contemporanei* (Collection of Manuscripts by Modern and Contemporary Authors) at the University of Pavia, established by Maria Corti; secondly, especially for letters and private papers, the *Fondo delle Carte di Famiglia* (Collection of Family Papers) in Carlo Levi's family home, now owned by his nephew Professor Giovanni Levi, at Via Bezzecca 11 in Turin; and thirdly, in the Harry Ransom Humanities Research Center at the University of Texas at Austin, the manuscript of *Cristo si è fermato a Eboli* (*Christ Stopped at Eboli*) is preserved.

In particular, it has been impossible to publish the vast collection of poems, which would have required the integration of two distinct collections, preserved in the *Fondazione Carlo Levi* (Carlo Levi Foundation) in Rome, and in the *Fondo Manoscritti* (Manuscript Collection) at Pavia, not yet available or ready for publication.

We should add, finally, that several of his private letters state that he was considering 'making a book' out of certain pieces of his journalism (not all of which are published in book form). We are referring to his reports from India and China, some of his investigations in southern Italy, and his 'pieces' on Rome and Italy.* The fact remains that Levi never did undertake any work towards the publication of the rich array of materials in his Collection. His rapid metaliterary references seem to us to be highly eloquent, and of course we have taken them into account, following his unintentional suggestions; but we have gone beyond them, of course, in our selection of 'publishable' material, we have gone in search of what were evidently the landmarks in his progress as an artist and a writer. That is to say, we have selected the organic and original aspects of his theoretical thought and his artistic career, in his most vital moments and in moments of transition toward other fields of endeavour, taking care primarily to gather all the richness and complexity of his cultural, artistic, and civil interests, and avoiding, where possible, overemphasis and repetition.

It goes without saying that it was not our intention to produce an unabridged edition of the writings, and only time will tell whether such an edition is needed. Our ambition was to offer these writings to the educated reader, enjoyable as individual texts, but also useful as substrate and as general context. We also hoped and primarily focused on the younger generations, so starved of 'past' and 'tradition', in order to allow them to discover the rich fabric of thought and study, passion and struggle, that lies beneath so many of the problems of the present day.

It was necessary to select in such a way as to remain faithful to the features of Carlo Levi's versatile personality, which was also cohesive and harmonious, endowed with a 'magnetic' positivity, a constructive faith in humanity, in a cyclical capacity for rebirth,

* See C. Levi and L. Saba, *Carissimo Puck. Lettere d'amore e d'amicizia*, edited by S. D'Amaro, Mancosu, Rome, 1994. (According to the Library of Congress, it is *Lettere d'amore e di vita.*)

even above and beyond the random elements of historical experience and the harshest moments of the crisis of modernity.

We have done our best to bring forth, through a wide-ranging exploration of his work, a complete and organic portrayal of the elements of a world in formation: his path as a writer and artist, his particular trajectory through the reality of our time, characterized unfailingly by a determined civic and political engagement. The various forms of expression of his idioms and the multiplicity of his interests did nothing to keep him from endowing us with Levi's unified and consistent view of the world. It is this richness that we wish to show the new generations.

Introduction

Eternal and Fleeting

by Giulio Ferroni

L'orologio (*The Watch*), by Carlo Levi, in the impassioned clarity with which it recounts the last days of the government of Ferruccio Parri and examines the collapse of the *azionista** approach that seemed to have gathered momentum from the Resistance, is one of the few books of the twentieth century in which you can palpably feel the 'breathing' of history, the 'air' and colour of a specific time, revealed spontaneously by the deeds and motions of the people, by the physical substance of the settings and material objects, and by what the people feel, in body and mind, in relation to these settings and objects. Levi's writing has the gift, nowadays sadly too often overlooked, of succeeding in giving a sense of life extending over time, of a space throbbing with presences, hopes, feelings, disappointments: and in *L'orologio* this time and this space are the time and space of Rome, a crowded, restive Rome, slothful and tumultuous, in disarray and riddled with glaring flashes, noises, and silences. *L'orologio* is like a novel,

* [*Translator's note.* A proponent of the anti-Fascist, pro-reform Partito d'Azione ('Action Party') founded in 1942.]

diary, or chronicle of the Rome of 1945, of a city in which the countless traces of the past, or its beauty and its decay, open out towards a new and uncertain world, welcoming and at the same time hindering its potential developments: in the deepest recesses of Rome are revealed the concreteness, the corporeality, the physicality of this vaguely defined progress towards something, towards open and interrupted possibilities, announced and frustrated, but always expected, as if coagulating in the air, in the mysterious echoes that spread through it. The opening of the book looks out precisely upon the mysterious breathing of Rome, as if it were possible to listen to its fascinating and menacing throbbing in the night:

> At night, in Rome, it seems you can hear lions roaring. There is an indistinct murmur, and that is the city breathing, amidst its dark domes and the distant hills, in shadow that glitters here and there; and every so often, the raucous noise of sirens, as if the sea were nearby, and ships were setting sail from the harbour for unknown horizons. And then there is that sound, both lovely and savage, cruel but not devoid of an odd sweetness, the roaring of lions, in the nocturnal desert of houses.
>
> I have never figured out what makes that sound. Perhaps hidden workshops, or car engines as they climb uphill? Or perhaps the sound is born, more than from any actual event, from the depths of memory, from the time when between the Tiber and the forests, on solitary slopes, wild beasts still roamed, and she-wolves still suckled foundlings?
>
> I listened carefully, peering into the dark, over roofs and terraces, into that world teeming with shadows; and the sound pierced me like a childhood memory, terrifying,

> moving, and obscure, bound up with another time. Even if produced by machinery, it is still an animalistic sound, which seems to well up from hidden viscera or from maws yawning futilely, seeking an impossible word. It is not the metallic sound of trams rounding bends in the night, the prolonged, thrilling screech of the trams of Turin, the doleful but confident howl of those factory-worker nights in the empty cold air. This is a noise full of laziness, like some yawning beast, indeterminate and terrible.
>
> You can hear it everywhere in the city. I listened to it for the first time, so many years ago now, as it came through the bars of a cell in the prison of Regina Coeli, along with the screams of the sick and the mad in the infirmary, and a distant clattering of metal; at the time it seemed like the breathing of that mysterious liberty that must somehow still exist, out there. And I was listening to it just now, a few months after the liberation, from a room high above the Via Gregoriana, a temporary, provisional refuge in those times of change, according to where a providential destiny led us, here and there.[1]

And the book concludes, again, with a night-time image of Rome, in which the author–narrator has just returned from Naples, after a car journey with the cabinet ministers Tempesti and Colombi (actually, Emilio Sereni and Attilio Piccioni); it is a double image, first viewed on the piazza in front of the main door of his block of flats, and then from the window of his flat:

> I stood there, alone, holding my suitcase, on the piazza, in front of the main door of my block of flats. The huge urban moon, riding high in the sky, leant down over the architecture like a mother. The paving shone brightly in the moonlight, compounded with silver: to one side, the

> oblique shadow of the church spread out the baroque profiles of saints upon the paving. Along the white pavement, a nightwatchman walked, dressed in black, like a scarab beetle. The facade of the block of flats was swept by moonlight, which picked out each cornice, each crack, each stone. Under the balcony, the carved angel, from her bat's lair, glowered out from beneath lowered brows.
>
> I crossed the threshold between the columns, walked through the atrium, and slowly climbed up the wide staircase, surrounded by statues. When I reached the top, I entered my flat.
>
> From the window, I heard the hour striking from a distant bell tower. I looked out. The city lay spread out, living, breathing, in the vague moonlight, with the indistinct noise of a forest full of ancient trees, barely stirring with the light breath of the breeze. I stood there listening, carefully, to that slightly murmuring silence, and I heard, coming from far away, from the streets or from the depths of memory the obscure sound of the night, the roaring of lions, like the echo of the sea in an abandoned seashell.[2]

To this process of listening to Rome, to its mysterious silence and its menacing noise, after *L'orologio* (in which beginning and end merge, in a circular fashion, in the roaring of the lions) Levi devoted the series of essays that are gathered in this volume, and which he himself intended to gather and publish with the title *Roma fuggitiva* ('Fleeting Rome'),[3] a name that had been inspired by the example of the verses of a Spanish poem dedicated to Rome, quoted by him in the unpublished addition to the article 'Il popolo di Roma' ('The People of Rome') and mistakenly attributed to Luis de Góngora (see p. 22 below); in reality, this is a sonnet by another great baroque writer, Francisco de Quevedo, and we reprint it here in its entirety:

A Roma sepultada en sus ruinas

Buscas en Roma a Roma ¡oh peregrino!
y en Roma misma a Roma no la hallas:
cadáver son las que ostentó murallas
y tumba de sí proprio el Aventino.

Yace donde reinaba el Palatino
y limadas del tiempo, las medallas
más se muestran destrozo a las batallas
de las edades que Blasón Latino.

Sólo el Tibre quedó, cuya corriente,
si ciudad la regó, ya sepultura
la llora con funesto son doliente.

¡Oh Roma en tu grandeza, en tu hermosura,
huyó lo que era firme y solamente
lo fugitivo permanece y dura![4]

'Roma fuggitiva' is also the title of a short note found among Levi's papers, dated 6 March 1963 (see p. 235 below): from the addition or preamble to the article 'Il popolo di Roma' and from this note, we learn that Levi took that reference as something like a metaphor for the endurance of that which history in any case had condemned to disappear, that is, that provisional 'restoration' that he had witnessed in the wake of the hopes of the Resistance. These are the words of the article:

> The 'fleeting moment' of Rome in these years is the external and evident history of the Italian ruling class, the fragile immobility of a restoration, the apathetic succession of scandals, speculations, deals, enrichments, the apparent triumph of a clerical bourgeoisie, and, flowing through the ruins, much like the river that so deeply moved the

> Spanish poet, is a glittering river of cars pounding the ancient roadways (p. 22).

And the note from 1963 distinguishes, on the one hand, between a Rome that is 'immense and pulpy' and, on the other hand, a 'living precious world', which seems to exist within it, consisting of a 'grey populace' waiting to speak, which is not 'dried out and dead like the stones and the architecture' and which seems to herald a possible world of the future. But, aside from the relatively optimistic view that Levi seems to take of the future, it is also true that the image of 'fleeting' Rome recapitulates within itself, for us, reading these pages today, after the many events and transformations in the way that the rest of the twentieth century played out, other, perhaps more nuanced impressions that can be taken from the words of the Spanish poet: as we read these articles, we sense that what was fleeting was not so much, or not only, the Rome of decay and neglect, of money-grubbing speculation, of 'boredom', but also the Rome of the 'commoners', in which Levi believed that he could discern the possibilities of a future 'with an ancient heart', and even the sweet and alluring Rome that he had known how to listen to so well, whose evocations and colours he has gathered for us, preserving all the signs, great and small, scenes of life in which we can find together all the times of so rich a history, perceived as 'nature', and a present that flows, which in its flight drags away with it the permanence of that history. For us, as we read today, the Rome of the fifties and the early sixties described by Levi is fleeting, too, because we have lost so many traces of it: and because the enduring *hermosura*, or beauty, of this city has endured new wounds and lacerations, because its features and its social life have changed even further, certainly with many positive aspects, but also with the loss of so many things, so much space, so much light, so much simple, elemental strength. Levi describes for us a Rome that we no longer see, and that we cannot see, even in the many places and in the many existences in which, despite everything, it persists, smothered as it is with cars, toxic emissions, artificial images, the models of mass culture, advertising, postmodern tourism: by now it has become a city to consume, a city to whisk through at top speed, it being impossible now to enter into the life of its stones, its corners and niches, still so wonderful, its gardens; in keeping with a destiny that is no longer only the destiny of Rome, but is now the destiny of the world, a world in which we are urged and trained to seize, to take, and in which it is increasingly difficult to listen, to hear in the midst of all the noise, the secret breathing of silence.

I do not think, however, that the reading of these pages must necessarily be a 'nostalgic' reading, even if a bit of nostalgia is inevitable (and certainly legitimate, in open defiance of those who insist that we must all chase constantly after the latest trend), especially for those who recall the appearance of Rome in the fifties and the early sixties, and who lived their early youth in those years. In fact, Levi does not merely fall under the simple spell of gathering the evocative charm of that Rome, still so marvellous, of immersing himself in its beating heart, but he also records its transformation in that crucial period of time, he tracks down the various signs of its becoming 'other', in the context of that radical mutation that Pasolini experienced in such a dramatic and lacerating fashion. The years described by these essays are precisely the years in which the humble Italy (an expression that was as dear to Levi as it was to Pasolini) began to move away from itself, while still revealing its traditional characteristics, the bright and dark sides of its 'common' life, and at the same time submitting, progressively and almost unawares, to the economic and consumer revolution that freed it from so much of the oppression of the past, and yet irrevocably transformed its face, slashing its stern beauty, destroying that 'peasant' civilization in which, specifically, Levi had believed that he could distinguish the path to a future that would be humane, free, and just.

In this process of transformation, Rome immersed itself with its capacity to incorporate within itself both conflicts and opposites, to convert change into continuity, to destroy while preserving, to contaminate, as it were, the times, mingling what passes with what endures: and with his descriptions and digressions on Rome, Levi succeeds in making us see precisely the physical substance of this change, of the fact that it is the product of a temporal interference. He exists, he moves, and he observes, precisely, in a fleeting Rome, within whose stability there vibrates a restless and ephemeral process of transformation; and in order to do this he makes use of his exceptional capacity to perceive the 'coexistence of times', of that 'way he has of hovering as if in some point in mid-air from which he can see the dials of the clocks sweeping in opposite directions' about which Italo Calvino wrote[5]: he remains immersed in the present, in what he recognizes as its 'heart', inside the organic body of Rome, but from there he is able to sense the echoes of its alluring and threatening past, which persists in its stones, in its streets, in its people, and the voices of the future on the march, both in what it rips apart, in the violations brought about by mass civilization, and in the positive possibilities which Levi can never bring himself to renounce.

His curiosity as an observer allows us to 'see' glimpses of concrete reality, of such total clarity, that they can truly 'redeem' for our memory both time and space in the very moment in which they are fleeing. This is a quality that distinguishes all of Levi's writing, both in the major works and in the essays and the journalism, and which we can trace back to that quest for happiness that always seems to guide him, even in the face of the harshest experiences and the most lacerating situations, back to his willingness to immerse himself in experiences, to feel the warmth of real places. An explanation of this gift of his can be found in the words that he himself wrote about his beloved Stendhal, in his 1960 preface to *Roma, Napoli e Firenzi* (*Rome, Naples and Florence*):

> Stendhal arrived in Italy in search of happiness, so ready to comprehend all things together, so receptive to everything, with mind, heart, and senses, that he immersed himself in it as if in a river of continual intellectual delight, greedy with a full and illuminating attention. He looks, he reasons, he observes, and above all he listens. His is a curious and acute ear, pressed against all the keyholes, and it seems that everything suits his choice, because he made it before things themselves. He was, perhaps, the first to understand the poetic value of the chance, of the peculiar, of the interrupted and partial and instantaneous, in the total simultaneity of an image.[6]

And, even if it is in his more relaxed and tranquil manner, with a vague serenity that may even strike us as unsettling, without any of the ruthless sense of adventure of the great Henri Beyle, Levi is truly 'so receptive to everything, with mind, heart, and senses', he plunges into the river of reality and listens to it with his 'curious and acute ear'; and in the way he knows how to listen, he also knows how to bring to light all of the 'value of the chance, of the peculiar, of the interrupted and partial and instantaneous, in the total simultaneity of an image.' And let us add only that his ability to give shape to the simultaneity of images constitutes the other great quality of his prose (and let us never forget that he was a painter!), perfectly parallel to that 'coexistence of times' discussed by Calvino.

The article that is closest to the time of *L'orologio* is 'Il popolo di Roma' (1951) – for which a preamble was written later, as mentioned above – which defines, with perhaps an occasional lapse of style, the very particular characters of the people of Rome, 'different from any other', the 'least rhetorical, least idolatrous, and least fanatical people on earth', their way of being ancient and adult; and it gazes with astonishment upon the fact that in Rome 'everything has already existed: and existence has not vanished into memory, rather it has remained present, in the houses, the stones, the people' (p. 7). In its authenticity, the lumpenproletariat of Rome seems to ward off those negative and dark characteristics, those sinister humours that weighed upon the Rome of *L'orologio*; it exorcizes the evil of the Rome described in a lecture of 1950, 'Il contadino e l'orologio' ('The Peasant and the Watch'), as the opposite of the two authentic 'capitals', Turin and Matera, and characterized as an 'eternal receptacle of history, bound up with eternal truths and institutions, outside real life and the development of daily life, with the eternal names of empire and church and the shapeless eternity of bureaucracy.'[7] But the qualities of this people are traced by Levi to their enduring link with the peasant world, which can be seen in the manifest form of the flocks of sheep that still move through the city:

> It preserves the flavour and customs of the country: it has been citified for countless generations and yet it is constantly being refreshed by a steady influx from the villages of Latium, following long-standing family ties, in keeping with the basically agrarian nature of the city where, although the Forum may no longer be the Campo Vaccino ('Field of Cows'), flocks of sheep are still herded by night through the streets of central Rome; and crickets chirp, tucked away in the massive cornices of the Palazzo

> Chigo, and thousands of birds settle, every evening, to sleep in the trees of Piazza Argentina, hidden among the branches, like wild fruit of the forest (p. 9–10).

The image of sheep moving across Rome is the living sign of an 'infinite synchronicity of time' (the 'coexistence of times' mentioned by Calvino): a sign to which Levi returns, not by chance, in a lovely article from 1955, 'La storia è presente' ('History is Present'), dedicated to the characters of Italy, in which he reminisces about the shepherd who actually 'crosses Rome, with his numerous and tranquil flock, amidst the cars deranged like so many mad sheep, and leads his flock to graze at the edge of the airport, even as it throbbed with the sound of engines.'[8] We should immediately note that in this return, a few years later, of the same image, there is a new feature of the coexistence of animals and machinery, that agrarian world to which they belong and the world of modernity and industry: and that in any case the cars themselves have now acquired animal characteristics ('deranged like so many mad sheep'), while the space of the 'airport' is contiguous with that of the pasture. And yet some years afterwards, 'La marrana e il morbillo' (1962; 'The Drainage Ditch and the Measles'), dedicated to the tragedy of three children who drowned in a drainage ditch and the general decay of the outskirts of Rome, would be obliged to acknowledge the dwindling of that coexistence; the ancient relationship of city and countryside now seems broken, the 'natural nature' has moved away, and all that can be seen of it are the occasional 'fragments and tatters':

> Just ten years ago, during the seasonal transhumance, shepherds drove flocks of sheep through the centre of Rome, as they moved down from the high mountain pastures to the lowland plains where they would winter their flocks. I remember watching them move by night through

> the Piazza del Pantheon, I remember hearing them from a distance as they passed in the shadows, like a muted murmur. And even then in the meadows of the Villa Doria Pamphili shepherds would spend the winter in their huts of straw and leafy branches. Nowadays, the much more numerous flocks of cars have occupied all the streets, making it impossible for animals to pass (p. 201).

The description that follows, of the decaying and provisional *borgata*, or grim peripheral quarter, where an 'expectant population' lives and waits, drapes a veil of disquiet over this evocation of a Rome that has moved away in so short a time from its roots in the countryside (and what indifferent tourist could believe today that just fifty years ago flocks of sheep were being herded across the Piazza del Pantheon?). And the disquiet endures, despite the conclusion of the article on a 'positive' note, glimpsing, in the account that the cleaning lady, Medea, offers of her own problems, a certain cheerful acceptance of life, the persistence of an 'absurd, innocent happiness'.

The cleaning lady is just one of the many predominantly 'common' characters who can be found in these pages: surfacing in these writings are, in effect, many moments of small lives, presented in their serene and measured clarity, at times with light and urbane humour, veined with indulgent sympathy. Consider, for instance, the beggar who comes to Levi's house periodically to ask for money, in 'Il potere dei poveri' ('The Power of the Poor'), and the mechanically inclined 'brothers' in 'La città dei fratelli' ('City of Brothers').

A serene and innocent cheerfulness pervades Levi's view of Rome in the fifties; he describes its places and occasions, amidst daily meetings, small and large events, absorbing their echoes and secret resonances. The memory retains the impact of the Roman festivities in 'La solitudine di Roma' (1955; 'The Solitude of Rome'): Levi is good at capturing the sense of atmosphere of these celebrations, speaking at the beginning of the article about the noises and sounds that vibrate in the city air:

> Indeed, we might say that festivals, at least the major festivals, in Rome, are sonorous and atmospheric, and are celebrated by noise and in the air. They are, in the final analysis, country festivals, and so, suddenly, and all at once, the city returns to what it was before the dawn of history: countryside and forest; and the machine-made sounds of the city give way to the cries of animals and the rustling of leaves (p. 27).

Festivities of dream and myth, whereby within the time of the city we find the time of what was there prior to the city; and precisely from this mythical point of view (and it would be too easy and simplistic to demonstrate its ideological limitations) emerges this magnificent approach to the Piazza Navona for the festivity of the *Befana*, or Epiphany:

> From afar, you can sense a sort of throbbing and shrilling in the air, and that alone begins to tug you towards a different world. The closer you come to the Piazza Navona, the greater this throbbing becomes, growing, little by little, into a vague, thundering, din, a continual chant, a chorus of countless sounds; and, as if by some absurd piece of magic, as you are swept into the crowd, it seems as if there is a rushing river in the broad lake of the piazza, the buildings, the churches, and the palaces all seem to vanish, and where a city once stood there is now nothing but a vast, primitive meadowland populated in the night by millions of crickets, all chirping together, in unison, in

> the looming shadow of the fields, beneath a black night sky (p. 29).

All the same, even the wonder of the Piazza Navona begins to shift, over the course of a few years: while the author continues to recognize in it 'a true mirror of the eternally unchanging', the disappearance of traditional toys and the invasion of Japanese toys ('I giocattoli giapponesi', 1962; 'Japanese Toys') introduces a suspicious mechanical aspect, the dangerous sense, marked by 'a subtle disdain', of a 'reduction of these objects', all the figures and characters of the toys, 'to machine-like qualities, to the point of absurdity.' And what can we say, after all the years that have gone by in the meantime, about the Piazza Navona of today and its *Befana*, by now completely stripped of any charm, suffocated by the clutter and bric-a-brac of the most stridently vulgar lumpen culture that observes in that piazza an empty, mechanical ritual, devoid now of any relationship with the festivities of long ago, with the festivities that Levi could still see and that Levi still loved so well?

And how many wonders we encounter in that Rome, so secretly inhabited by something so profoundly ancient, by the enduring myth that Levi is constantly seeking out, civil and cordial divining rod that he is! And so behold the 'Passeggiata domenicale' (1955; 'Sunday Stroll'), with the vision of the puppet theatre of Pulcinella, or Punch, at the Pincio.[9] Behold the discovery of the city from on high, in the helicopter flight ('L'elicottero', 1956; 'The Helicopter'). Behold the 'Apparizioni a Roma' (1957; 'Apparitions in Rome') that Rome conjures forth from its breast, 'actual, living, substantial, specific, colourful apparitions: real things that become apparitions, you might say, precisely because of their remarkable realness, their abundant quality of existence' (p. 53). Behold the gunshots and the shattered crockery of New Year's Eve, with the custom of tossing out old things, in full recognition of all their symbolic value, leading to a confrontation with the presence of death, both in terms of the insults levelled against time ('Ammazzare il tempo', 1958; 'Killing Time'), and in terms of the scorn for objects and their durability ('Le tarme', 1961; 'Clothes Moths'). Behold, in 'Piante e semi' (1958; 'Plants and Seeds'), the humanity of the owner of a tiny shop in the Piazza Navona, and his wife, 'the mistress of a tiny, unshakeable world, unchanging over time, an indissoluble and eternal fragment of the humble Italy, which asks for nothing, and just goes on living, in its peacefulness' (p. 107). Behold, moving festively through the streets of the centre of Rome, girls in their work clothes during the lunch hour, in the splendour of springtime ('Ragazze e alberi', 1959; 'Girls and Trees'). And behold the allure of the empty, silent city, from which Levi extracts sensations of intimate and secret happiness, almost as if, with the dwindling of its customary bustle and crowds, the beauty of the urban fabric had succeeded in accommodating within itself its ego, as if it became almost one with it, eliminating distances and artifices, rediscovering the deep breathing of nature, an original uncontaminated unity. Thus the 'Elegia di Ferragosto' (1957; 'Elegy to the Mid-August Holidays') tracks the action of silence, which revives 'the deep past', which is able to 'reveal a naked and solemn nature', in which everything becomes, in fact, nature, with colonnades that have reverted to 'forest', churches to 'grottoes': and it immerses the writer in a happy solitude, allows him to come into contact with 'the arcane world of memory; the changeless shell of things' (p. 70). If we are reminded of the mid-August holidays of Rome in Nanni Moretti's film *Caro diario* (*Dear Diary*), we also cannot fail to note how different from Levi's, how much less 'ancient', perhaps more 'postmodern', is the effect that the actor-director obtains as he moves through the city, reaching its extreme limits on his moped, followed by the camera. Again, the mid-August holidays of Rome are the subject of the article 'Le città vuote' (1958; 'The Empty Cities'), which compares the emptiness of *Ferragosto* with that of 'that dawn hour when everything is shut up and motionless in the grey light. Even the houses seem like so many sleeping birds, and anyone who, all alone, is awake and on the move is the new master of all space' (p. 122): but here the mid-August holidays no longer appear as a return of the city to its past or towards nature, but rather as a ritual of abandonment, 'with certain funereal implications', a way of punishing the city for its bond with work and exhaustion, of abandoning it 'to the vendetta of the sun' (p. 124). But the allure of the empty city returns in all its precision in 'Un'alba a Roma' (1959; 'A Dawn in Rome'): here what holds sway is the evocative juxtaposition of distant and far-off animal songs at first light, which the author hears after a night hard at work, completing his book on Germany in the park of the Villa Strohl-Fern; and as he listens he begins to experience that sensation, so often sought and so often attained by Levi, that he 'was at the heart of things', that he had captured a mysterious happiness created precisely by this immersion in the obscure foundation of nature itself.

And Levi knew how to derive a sense of happiness from public events as well, events of great power in the new mass culture, such as the landing of Lunik 2 on the moon ('La luna nuova', 1959; 'The New Moon'), to which he offers an optimistic interpretation, making it into an image of the overcoming of a limit and the opening of a new form of communication, or the 1960 Olympics, to which he devoted the two articles 'Un bambino che vola' ('A Child in Flight') and 'Dopo la festa' ('After the Party'). But the subject of sport is also touched by the repartee on Roma's relegation to the second division in 'Il popolo di Roma' and by the amusing 'Calcio e letterati' (1962; 'Football and Men of Letters'). In the Olympics and in the presence of so many athletes in Rome, Levi even perceives 'the physical and visible appearance of happiness' (and he presents two different images of this happiness in the athletes Wilma Rudolph and Livio Berruti): and he bestows upon us the memory of a still 'home-made' world of sports, not coldly programmed, not yet amplified in the gigantic media and promotional machine that is killing it, and of a Rome that still succeeded in experiencing that event in a 'folksy' manner, as if it were an ancient festivity.

In the second of his essays on the Olympics, however, as in almost all his writings of the early sixties (but already in 'Lo scalino di Roma', 1958; 'The Steps of Rome'), in the midst of all his enthusiastic participation, we also begin to see the signs of the ills that are assailing this city and its 'common' life: its progressive decay, under the hammer blows of speculation and corrupt politics, of a hasty and ignorant modernity. We see the construction of the Hilton hotel, which once and for all defaces Monte Mario; we see the determination and the renewed aggression of the Italy of *luigini,** which continues to spin 'its web of privilege and self-interest'; we see the damage to the face of Rome that was done by the construction of the Via Olimpica. In the article 'Il labirinto' (1962; 'The Labyrinth'), the establishment of one-way streets with new routes for traffic offers material for his reflection on the 'loss of existential confidence' triggered by the change in the relationship with the physical places of the city, by the obligation to reduce all movement to a 'programme'; the modern need to regulate traffic seems to Levi to contradict the very spirit of Rome, in which the 'haphazard' and random are essential:

* [*Translator's note.* A term coined by Levi to denote a political lackey who inflicts cruel treatment on the poor and weak, while fawning upon the wealthy and powerful. It originated with the character of the Fascist mayor of Gagliano, Don Luigino Magalone, who featured in his book *Cristo si è fermato a Eboli* (1945; *Christ Stopped at Eboli*). The term *luigino* (plural *luigini*) appears in several of Levi's books.]

> Life thus becomes, necessarily, a programme, an advance decision, from the very beginning. And since, in Rome, those who move about tend to follow opportunities, and want to live in the city, and not merely move from place to place, and stop to see and be seen, and shift moods and directions, the advance choice is in conflict with the nature of the city, with its very form, which is the expression of creative fantasy. Upon this historical and poetic structure of imagination and free human thought that is the city of Rome, an abstract choice becomes the violent crystallization of formless chaos: labyrinth (p. 217–218).

Today we know that it could not be any different: that modernity and our deranged dependence on cars have once and for all condemned us to the labyrinth,[10] that in order to enjoy the centre of the city, its places and its occasions, we must first of all enter the labyrinth, run through its diversions and detours, without even taking into account the fact that that very city centre is still plagued by the mopeds that dangerously zip and zoom, even across traffic islands. We know that almost all of our movements wind up conflicting with 'the nature of the city', that a labyrinth is inevitable, and that Rome is caught in a vice-like grip that each one of us is helping to tighten around its heart: we also know that, the way things are now, it would be neither possible nor fair to drive around carelessly, at whim. But what is certain, in any case, is that Levi's considerations, here and in many points, remind us and make us think about what we have lost, about the Rome that we no longer possess.

We also know that politics played a not insubstantial role in this loss: and in these articles there emerge images, few in number but strikingly vivid, including that of an address delivered by Giulio Andreotti in the Piazza del Popolo ('Sostanza e accidente', 1960; 'Substance and Chance'), which explores the 'anthropological' aspect of political relationships, of the consensus that the Christian Democrats have with the masses, of the need to act with respect to that consensus. It is likely, however, that to view things with hindsight, the role played by politics was not even that essential and crucial: it was through and above and beyond politics that those anthropological signs imposed themselves, that profound configuration of social and environmental relationships, which Levi depicted with such exemplary clarity in the stories of *L'orologio*, and of which he supplies here yet other manifold aspects. Perhaps it is Rome itself that must accept the responsibility for its own loss, for its own fleeting dissolution; but aside from any responsibility, there is an overall context that acted upon it and that nowadays we know as globalization, and which Rome could never of course have escaped. In his love of the humble Italy, Levi largely overlooked this context: he simply subsumed it in a general 'pursuit of happiness', he perhaps hoped that international exchanges would offer a broader scope and a renewed vitality to that 'peasant' world view, that it truly would lead to a recovery of the world's 'ancient heart'.

In spite of everything, in spite of all the transformations and the disintegrations that he saw affecting the fabric of Rome, Levi maintained his loyalty to the positive image of the Roman 'people': indeed, the events of July 1960, when that people fought at Porta San Paolo against the Tambroni government (see the addition or preamble to 'Il popolo di Roma' and the article 'San Lorenzo e San Paolo', or 'San Lorenzo and San Paolo'), gave him bright new hopes; and his enduring love of the vitality and authenticity of that Roman people can still be clearly seen in the article that was not published at the time, devoted to a piece of city news from 1962, which also aroused the indignation of Piovene and Pasolini ('Un ragazzo che rubava autoradio a Piazza Navona', or 'A Boy Steals a Car Radio in the Piazza Navona').

Carlo Levi died a few months before Pasolini did, and he never saw, or never chose to see, the infernal Rome of his younger friend, who took part on 20 October 1974 in the round table following Levi's exhibition at the Palazzo Te in Mantua:[11] he was not obliged to face up to the demise of that people and its ancient heart, with its progressive submission to the yoke of the models of television and advertising; he never even came close to glimpsing the horrors and degradation of Rome of Pasolini's *Petrolio*. The city that he describes for us in these articles, even though it is obliged to deal with the many signs that threaten it, that drive him to engage in polemics that are in any case charged with civil tension, still preserves within it a confident equilibrium between past and present, offering those who live there the gift of its stunning beauty, the skill with which it succeeds in allowing the coexistence within it of different and distant times, multiple and clashing images (the coexistence of times and the simultaneity of images, to be precise: and it would be interesting to compare this fleeting Rome with the city depicted in black and white by some neo-realist films). For us, this Rome remains a potential unachieved: a city that, given its special relationship between its past and a possible future, contained within itself great promises of equilibrium and civilization, cut short by chaotic and destructive development, by the Italy of bureaucracy, business, and corruption, the Italy of those who in *L'orologio* had been described as *luigini*, or political lackeys, and by a reckless use of modernity. In the final analysis, its destiny was the same as an Italy that, at a certain point in its history (the watershed of the sixties) seemed to be about to find the paths of a 'human' modernity, reconciled with its past, an open and pluralistic democracy, and instead lost them, hurling itself into the abyss of a pointless and greedy postmodernity.

As we read these 'Roman' articles (like the articles on Italy collected in *Le mille patrie*, or 'The Thousand Homelands') we truly regain the sense of an endangered 'marvel': it is precisely Levi's capacity for observation and listening, his sense of time and colour, his human cordiality, his 'humanism', that eludes the disintegration and the deconstruction of the 'negativity' of the twentieth century, that preserves for us, as if intact, this wonderful Rome, the image of this great and fragile city, at once eternal and fleeting, that in those difficult years knew better than it does today how to win our love, and possessed an authenticity and a gentleness that have perhaps long since vanished (and yet, in spite of everything, still remains the most beautiful city on earth!). Even now, at this great distance, in a world that has followed paths so different from those he foretold and in which he believed, the doctor-painter-writer invites us to recognize, even today, traces, fragments, corners, and visions of that 'wonder': he reminds us of our responsibility for 'taking care of' and affectionately guarding that which still survives, the duty to refrain from lacerating it any further, to 'save' it and allow it to live, and not merely as a cultural and touristic 'asset', for ourselves and for the world.

G. F.
Rome, April 2002

Translator's Note

by Antony Shugaar

Like an Advent calendar set in Rome instead of Bethlehem, in which each panel opens on to a glowing, delicately framed vignette in the style of Fellini or Rossellini, Carlo Levi's essays combine a childlike sense of wonder and enchantment with a very adult sense of detachment and technique.

The thirty-three essays are 'Letters from Rome', written by a northern Italian author for a newspaper published in the northern city of Turin, and they span nearly a decade. They portray a Rome that at the time had a glow of timeless individuality, and, to the present-day reader, a Rome that seems like the lost capital of a lost Italy. And yet it remains, recognizably, Rome: an endless succession of unique, ephemeral characters.

If there is a single representative hero in this collection of essays, it is surely the clerk of the Ministry of Finance, who shows up at the office every morning, and then trots downstairs to spend a day cycling through the farmland and forest around Rome in search of fresh wild asparagus. This he trades for dinner or a bottle of wine at Levi's local *osteria*. This clerk is an ideal employee, notes Levi: he takes up no room, and he causes no trouble. In a fitting coda to this loving and comic portrayal, when he finally retires from his position at the ministry, he stops gathering asparagus, which was his real work.

The clerk embodies the quirky reverse logic of Rome and of southern Italy in general. He is like the beggar in another essay who tells his would-be benefactor, 'Your Excellency, you live too far away. Find yourself another beggar.'

I have done my best to translate this 'lost world' into English. It is a series of points of view: a letter from Rome, written for a readership in the north; a letter from an Italy that no longer exists, written by someone who was keenly aware of the threatening, onrushing modernity (best exemplified by the construction of the new Hilton hotel, and the appearance of Japanese toys on the stalls of the traditional market of San Giovanni). I did not know the Rome that Levi described, some 50 years ago. But the Rome (and the Italy) that I first encountered has vanished: an Italy in which you walk down the street in the evening and hear the sound of a single football match or opera being broadcast on hundreds of television sets tuned to one of two or three available channels. Modernity, here, continues to be conjugated in a distinctly Roman form, despite all of Levi's fears of levelling and loss of identity.

Lurking amidst the nostalgia for the old we find the beginning of a new resistance, the premonitory rumblings (chapters XXI and XXIX) of what would be a long season of grim death and grief, the period of terrorism known as the Years of Lead. These were the years that would kill off so much of a Rome and an Italy that are now gone forever. And yet, Rome springs eternal, endlessly quirky and interesting.

And, at his most lyrical, Levi evokes a city of magical realism, a city that still exists, whether it is in the dark alleys of the early morning, when a lorry loaded with a swaying, swollen cargo of dark red balloons inches its way downhill, rumbling and then vanishing into the shadows, or in the crystalline windswept light of afternoon, when a helicopter rises, roaring, into the air, hovering like 'a soap bubble that a child releases into the air…the drone of the spinning blades' working on the imagination.

CHAPTER I

The People of Rome

One of the 47 million living Italian poets and versifiers (according to the latest census figures) wrote the following odd little quatrain about the people of Rome. I chanced upon it in my reading and, though it hardly shines as a piece of literary composition, and by no stretch of the imagination is the author a Belli, it still contains a kernel of truth:

> The People of Rome are a *Populusque*
> with family ties to Senate and Curia
> and will endure for centuries, *quousque*
> the last drop has been drained.

That last drop, I think, refers to the wine of the Castelli; unless the poet was alluding, metaphysically, to the last drop of time, the end of the ages, which the Romans, with agreeable nonchalance, would thus polish off, like a bottle of wine. Perhaps the latter interpretation is bold and even contrived; but however we choose to read these verses, either version makes perfectly good sense. After all, they both amount to the same thing. Let us consider that the Romans alone know how to withstand, with the same unshakeable equilibrium, both the deceitful and oppressive venom of their wine and the no less burdensome and venomous deceptions of time. Let us further consider that, accustomed as they are to that wine from time immemorial, they have adapted to it, developing an immunity, blunting its sting through the passage of time, just as they have employed the virtues of that wine to blunt time's sting. And in that wine, they have drowned all time together, along with all their ancient past, all their glory and poverty.

This people, the poet tells us, is a 'populusque'. That is, a people different from any other, set apart precisely by that suffix, that conjunction, the basis of its claim to nobility, which can be seen written everywhere, on ruins, pediments, stelae, and even on the *fontanelle*, or little public drinking fountains. This *que* constitutes its assertion of nobility, which aristocrats place before their names, while the Roman populace bears it proudly after its name, like a silk train or the multicoloured tail of an exotic bird. From the outset, the Roman populace has always been fastened, as it were, inseparably to something else: the senate, the government, and the church, serving as a necessary appendage, a vernacular translation. It has always existed as a function of the senate, the government, and nothing more. It is the creature, the mollusc that lives within the magnificent baroque seashell that is Rome: that scrollwork, that colour, that exquisite mother-of-pearl is its home, its shell. The people of Rome see Rome only from within, treat Rome without formality, wear Rome like a comfortable old suit of clothes, and since they alone do not see the city's exterior, they alone are untouched by Rome's rhetoric. The Lord knows that Rome's rhetoric is perhaps unequalled in its sheer mass, perhaps as boundless as its grandeur, the image of that 'goddess Roma', of whom it may be said that 'those who fail to acknowledge you/have minds enveloped in chilly shadow/and in their felonious hearts, slowly buds/the wood of Barbary',[1] to quote the words of another, greater Italian poet and a surrealist in spite of himself. The common people of Rome feel at home in that Dea Roma, Rome the goddess. They stroll across her skin, eat and sleep among her tresses, enjoy the cool evening breezes upon her back. They are her tenant, her subtenant, and her landlord as well. They take in her flavours and aromas; they are, we might say, a part of her. For that very reason, however, they are not inclined to respect, much less admire, this deity, and therefore neither respect nor admire any of the other possible deities, by definition inferior to the deity upon whom they carelessly recline, minding their own business or perhaps making love.

The people of Rome, privy to and almost part of the daily life of the heavenly gods, are equally familiar with the earthly powers, all because of that little assertion of nobility, the *que* that serves as their tail. Other peoples in other cities have often been servants and occasionally masters, and they have organized themselves around and laboured upon matters unrelated to the exercise of power: commerce, navigation, manufacture, the arts, farming. But the common folk of Rome have never, or almost never, been either servants or masters. They have never, or almost never, dabbled in the trades or the arts. They have lived with the lords, in their palaces and in their churches, working freely for them, driving their carriages to and fro, preparing their meals, improving their manners, dressing them, amusing them, and at the same time amusing themselves. In other words, the populace of Rome has always been a necessary complement to power, whether that power took the form of the Roman Senate, Empire, Church, Monarchy, or Republic. Having long been on speaking terms with consuls, popes, cardinals, princes, governors, cabinet ministers, and managing directors, it has come to think of them as equals, taking their measure as ordinary men and growing impervious to the intimidation attendant upon power. This constant proximity has meant that the difference between a Roman lord and a Roman commoner truly must be sought, for the most part, in clothing and wealth. There is no way to tell a Roman prince from his coachman in the way that they think, act, or behave, in their emotions or their appearance or their features. The prince looks like a coachman and the coachman looks like a prince (assuming that we are talking about a real prince and a real coachman, both of which are quite rare, to tell the truth). And the two crossed keys, one silver and the other gold, the white key and the yellow key, which for ordinary men open earthly and heavenly gates, are so familiar to the common folk of Rome that they think of them as nothing more than the keys to their own home.

That home, the city of Rome, is the most beautiful place on earth, an endless spectacle of architecture, forms, colours, and images from every period, in which a boundless genius seems to have taken crystalline shape. The people who live there, then, have become indifferent to all this beauty, a beauty that has made, and will continue to make, so many hearts race with real and feigned raptures.

And for that reason, this is the least rhetorical, least idolatrous, and least fanatical people on earth (it is no accident that in Roman dialect, or *romanesco*, the term *fanatico* means 'crazy'). Not even time stirs or frightens them, because time itself lies in a pile just outside their door, within reach, since Rome is the very image of time, the endlessly synchronous. This people, then, free of all internal fear of, or yearning for, state and power, church and religion, time with its glory and grandeur, universal ideas (which have certainly resided here), and beauty itself, has earned itself a reputation for scepticism and indifference. Though all these things seem alien to the Roman people, deep down they possess them: their gestures, their actions, their very faces brim with oratorical force, ancient greatness, an understanding of power; their words are the words of kings, princes, and cardinals; and all their motions possess a natural beauty. In them, everything has become physical, concrete: they are an ancient people, full-grown, free of the trappings of youth, without a hint of romanticism. Likewise, Belli, the poet of Rome, is the least romantic, the most adult, the most imposingly tragic of all Italian poets.[2]

Here, everything has already existed: and existence has not vanished into memory, rather it has remained present, in the houses, the stones, the people: a remarkable welter of times and differing conditions that resolves into an absolute simplicity of emotion and interest. It has all been done before: only death is still to come ('and it all ends in hell').[3] The virtues are not the moral and ideological values (which the passage of too long a time has gradually flattened out), but simpler and more visible values: health, physical strength, knowing how to eat and drink, knowing how to speak with a certain humour and brevity, knowing how to command respect, sincerity, friendship. For a people free of complexes and moralism, all possible human conditions are understandable, acceptable, and normal. It is a normal condition of humanity to be poor, debt-ridden, in trouble with the law, for your wife to cheat on you: it is natural to be a drunk and no guilt attaches to drunkenness; it is natural to be a convict (the most classic Roman folk lament runs: 'In the prison of Regina Coeli there is a staircase/if you never climb it, you are no Roman/No Roman and not even from Trastevere'). Underlying all these conditions is man and his simplest, most basic value: the courage to live. One evening, I happened to stop for an espresso in a cafe in Piazza Argentina; the football championship matches were still being played, but the impending defeat of the Roma football team had been in the air for some time now. The cafe in question had long been a meeting place for fans and supporters of that exquisitely working-class team. Every day, for months, the customers of that bar had kept up a running banter with the owner about their beloved, endangered team: from first thing in the morning to last thing at night, there was an incessant volley of gibes, jokes, impassioned debates. That evening, an old man came

The people of Rome … wear Rome like a comfortable old suit of clothes … untouched by Rome's rhetoric.

in to buy a cigar; he was dressed in a threadbare raincoat, with a peaked cap on his head: a horse-drawn carriage driver or a taxi driver. He too began to make jokes about the Roma team: 'Roma is going to be relegated to the B series, the second division,' he said. 'The next thing you know, they'll be playing against a lousy team like Fortitudo, against schoolboys. In my block of flats, there is a nice big courtyard: the Roma team can come and play there, and I can just watch the matches from my window.' And more banter of this sort. The owner answered, 'Just you wait, the championship isn't over yet, and we will come out on top. Obviously you are a Lazio fan!' The old man immediately changed both tone and subject, saying, 'I'm not a Lazio fan and I'm not a Roma supporter; I was just teasing, because everybody else is doing it in here. I barely know who Roma and Lazio are, I don't understand sports, I have never been to a football match, I have never even bet on a football match. I don't pay any attention at all to these games, I don't know them. I have spent my time on other games. When I was seven years old (and you know this very well) my mother and father died: I began to play at life. Then I went off to be a soldier: seven years at war, four wounds, three medals (who knows why): I had to play at war. I came back permanently disabled: I couldn't have children, but it turns out that according to the public records I have kids (they were my wife's). What can you do? I played at having a family. Then, for the rest of my life, I played with hunger and poverty: and I always lost. Now I am an old man, I am sixty-five years old and there is only one game left to play, the game of death. I am ready to lose at that game and lose immediately: but I can't seem to pull it off. If I could just figure out how to lose that game, if I could die, I would be a happy man. I would go straight to heaven (and that is certainly where I would go) and I would say to the bloke up there, "Here I am. Why don't you go down there for a while and take my place; see what it's like to live in the city."'

That was how the old carriage driver talked, like a character out of Shakespeare, with the bitter irony of someone who, having long since rejected all illusions and appearances, finds himself alone with life, in a bare and very real world, in which a man can speak frankly even to the bloke up there.

This people, then, is different from any other, by its nature and its history, and is fully aware of it, with a certain ironic pride. I am talking about the original people of Rome, only a fairly small number of the inhabitants of the city; those who have always lived in the old quarters, in the neighbourhoods of the city centre, the true Rome, Roman and papal. They are mostly artisans, of all sorts: carpenters, blacksmiths, framers, plumbers, cobblers, pastry cooks, confectioners, glass-makers, garage workers, mechanics, porters, and so on; and large and small traders, ranging from street sellers of green olives and sweets, roasted chestnuts (or boiled chestnuts, the poor man's roasted chestnuts), or holy images, to the owners of garish shops or bars competing for the brightest array of neon lights and the most modern furnishings, butchers, tavern owners, waiters, and small-time landlords; and carriage drivers who bring their horses, every evening, to the stables in Trastevere, down little lanes fragrant with the earthy odour of the stalls, and taxi drivers and lorry drivers and tram drivers and conductors, and street sweepers; and tour guides, and deacons, and custodians of holy sites and ruins and museums; and professionals and, of course, the employees of the ministries and the thousands and thousands of government and semi-private agencies. This people with its countless minor vocations lives in the historic section of Rome, from Trastevere to St Peter's, to Piazza del Popolo, around the various basilicas, and stretching out into the newer neighbourhoods, along the ancient roads leading into the city, out towards the countryside. It preserves the flavour and customs of the country: it has been citified for countless generations and yet it is constantly being refreshed by a steady influx from the villages of Latium, following long-standing family ties, in keeping with the basically agrarian nature of the city where, although the Forum may no longer be the Campo Vaccino ('Field of Cows'), flocks of sheep are still herded by night through the streets of central Rome; and crickets chirp, tucked away in the massive cornices of the Palazzo Chigi, and thousands of birds settle, every evening, to sleep in the trees of Piazza Argentina, hidden among the branches, like wild fruit of the forest. This people of city dwellers is, at the same time, a people of the countryside, in tastes, customs, way of thinking. Its favourite pastimes are walks in the countryside, festivals at the Castelli with the new wine; the chief form of exercise is still hunting: young overweight men, lazy and apathetic, get up before dawn and ride out on their Vespas, to climb over mountains and down valleys in quest of elusive birds.

I often used to dine in an unassuming eatery, or *osteria*, near the Fontana delle Tartarughe, at the entrance to the Ghetto. The food was excellent and wholesome, but the owners refused to serve rice because, they said, they had eaten so much rice when they were in the military that they refused to allow that soldierly food into their kitchen. Until last year, you could order seasonal wild asparagus, which was a stunning green and very aromatic, as fresh as can be, much better than the asparagus that you could find at the market. I asked the owners where they managed to find such fragrant vegetables. 'They are freshly picked,' they told me. 'An employee of the Ministry of Finance brings them to us.' This clerk, they explained to me, spent his days as follows: every morning, he would go into the ministry for a few minutes, to establish his existence and presence. Then he would climb on to an old bicycle he owned and ride out to the countryside, along the Via Salaria and the Via Flaminia, where he would pass the rest of the day hunting asparagus by the sides of the fields. He knew all the right places, and he would gather as much as two or three kilos. In the other seasons, he was satisfied with gathering mushrooms or wild chicory. In the evening, he would return to town with his booty, which he would sell to the tavern owners, or else he would trade it for dinner or wine. He was a perfect employee, taking up no extra space in the overcrowded offices of the ministry and creating no complications or public scandals for the public in exchange for his salary, but simply and peacefully pursuing his innocent and Rousseauistic love of nature. Unfortunately, last year this model employee reached compulsory retirement age; and of course he promptly stopped going out to hunt this choice asparagus. He was retired now and he rightly felt that he no longer had to do this work either, as it had been his true job as an employee of the Ministry of Finance.

Another civil servant, a doorman at a ministry, whom I often run into late at night, in a cafe, taught me what he calls the secrets of hunting, especially how to kill large animals, such as a wild boar, a cow, or even a rhinoceros, with, say, a no. 2 shotgun cartridge. When you cut perforations all around it, 'it will punch out a bathtub.' The doorman also goes out to look for mushrooms: his latest adventure, last month, was this. Looking for mushrooms in the forest, he found a purse instead, with 120 lire in it, one 100-lire coin and two 10-lire coins, along with the owner's address. He returned the purse to the housekeeper who had lost it; she was grateful and asked how she could repay him for the trouble. 'Let's go back together to where you lost the purse,' the doorman answered, half in jest, because the woman was not particularly attractive or sexually desirable. 'Gladly,' she replied. 'When would you like to go?' 'Tomorrow,' the doorman told her, 'but you can wait. No woman is to be despised, but I'm fifty years old and I can do better; if I had no one better, I'd be satisfied with you. As far as the rest are concerned, my wife can't complain. She never found me in the hospital or at the police station. And if, now and then, I have done some bad things, I never did anything wrong to her; she can be happy.' Who would ever guess, observing from the outside, that these doormen, clerks, and civil servants could entertain such idyllic and agrarian sentiments? Who can truly understand the heart of a Roman civil servant? Another doorman, from the Ciociaria, with a sharp-eyed sunburnt peasant's face, permanently disabled and awarded the silver medal for his acts of heroism during the First World War, sang the praises of fear to me as we sat with a quarter-litre of wine. 'Can you tell me why I was given the medal? I don't have the slightest idea, myself. All I know is that every three months I get 230 lire, but I really don't know why. There were seven of us, all of us fools, up in the Trentino, we were thirsty and we went to get water in the middle of all that snow. We were scared, let me tell you! I caught a bullet in the head and I never knew what hit me. The other six fools were dead and I got a medal, who knows why. The disability? That happened on the Montello: I was up a true service tree, acting as lookout, and a triple-impact mortar round landed. I woke up eight days later in hospital. They had stolen my wallet, my pocket scissors, my stamps, my prepaid postcards, my jackknife, and all the rest of my kit. The only courage is the courage of fear.' These were pretty much the same sentiments that I had heard from the waiter Giacinto, who boasted of his cowardice and took pride in it, as I described in *L'orologio* (*The Watch*). And yet this same doorman, who spoke with such scorn and humour, was still strangely proud of the antiquity of his stock: 'I am an Ernico, from Piglio; I descend from the Ernici, seven centuries before Rome. I may be a country bumpkin, from the Ciociaria, but we were there seven centuries before Rome, we built Rome.'

The glory of antiquity has none of the rhetoric of grandeur or of the empire. It is an almost physical glory, like the glory of having strong muscles, being in good health, living to a great age (as if the past were long-lived, an indicator of good historical health). I ran into one of the renowned fishmongers of Campo dei Fiori, white-haired, with the lean erect posture of a racing cyclist. His face was proud and daring; he had a large classical nose and elongated features, like one of the Roman busts in the Museo del Campidoglio. 'I come of Roman stock, true Roman stock, going back who knows how many generations,' he told me. 'As you see me, I am sixty-four, and, as a man, I am an athlete. A true Roman, let me tell you; never been sick in my life. My wife (I am a widower) was a true Roman woman, she died without an injection, in a matter of minutes. Her blood pressure was high, 200, ready to blow. What a woman! You should have seen her, long-limbed, dark, a real Roman woman; they named her Queen of the Arenula, in 1911 (my sister was a princess). She turned it down because I was in the army. I know everyone in Rome, Trilussa was a friend of mine.' One of his pals, who, as always happens in these *osteria* chat-fests, had been pushing him to talk, suddenly contradicted him: 'So what?' 'I sell fish, my dad sold fish, and that's what he knew how to do. I want to tell you the truth. It doesn't cost me a cent to tell the truth.' 'Okay, so then what?' 'So nothing, after the truth, there's nothing more to say.' All the virtues of the people of Rome could be found in the words of the fishmonger: antiquity, strength, health, art, and authenticity. Physical strength is the prime virtue of a people that has managed to attain simplicity by dint of complexity. It is common to see trophies and athletic medals, displayed in shops and *osterie* as their winner's proudest achievement. In a little *osteria* in Traste-

This clerk … would go into the ministry for a few minutes, to establish his existence and presence. Then he would … ride out to the countryside … where he would pass the rest of the day hunting asparagus by the sides of the fields.

vere there is a large framed photograph of the owner holding five sacks of wheat on his back and friends standing on top of the sacks of wheat. The owner's son is, in turn, a boxer and a motorcyclist, pursuits more in keeping with modern times. There are amateur fast-walkers and marathon runners, often unemployed men, who would win world-class competitions if the prize was a sizzling steak. And then first and foremost is the collective love of motorcycles, Lambrettas, Vespas, and mopeds. This love, disastrous for our ears and tranquillity, is common to every other city in Italy and arises from a confluence of diverse motives, including a taste for virility, noise, and self-affirmation (and perhaps, as I have said elsewhere, a deviant and machine-driven variant on lycanthropy). But in Rome there is a bias towards the more physical aspects: the sense of pure noise, high speed, and especially the passion for strength and agility. If you see the amazing feats of balance performed by Roman common folk, riding a Vespa three at a time, or four at a time, or five, you will surely admit that the renowned cowboys of the American plains have met their match.

The virtues of eating and drinking are not merely virtues of gluttony; *pagliata* ('calf's intestines') and spaghetti alla carbonara and Frascati wine; above all they are social virtues, a profound appreciation of company, human interaction, friendship, which is held sacred above all things by the common folk of Rome. The *osterie* are the true gathering spots, the places for get-togethers and true friendship, the centre of life, and you sense a cordial, friendly, balanced, and welcoming atmosphere. There is a complex shared life in the *osterie*, a mutual familiarity, an absence of false hierarchies, a level of tolerance, a simple and profound bond between men, which even finds its own forms of organization. Everywhere, there are associations, societies, and clubs, based in an *osteria*, whose organizational purpose seems basically to be for the members to dine together. These clubs are of two kinds: associations for interest, as they are called, and associations for fun. In both cases, the members pay set weekly dues. In the associations for interest, the dues are used for business loans to the members, and the interest from the loans is used to subsidize group meals. In the associations for fun, the dues are devoted solely to the preparation of club meals, which occur once or a number of times a year. There are a great many of these associations of food-loving friends: in the quarter of Trastevere alone, it seems that there are more than one hundred and fifty. Some of the clubs are for women: powerful matrons, businesswomen, and shopkeepers for the most part, who get together for marathon dinners and drinking sessions, with all the violent cheer, freedom of language, and terrifying power of a matriarchal society. At the Antica Pesa, a restaurant known for its fine cuisine and the friendliness of the owners, the 'Smaniosi' of Trastevere, a club founded in 1902, meets regularly to consume a vast meal, in a sacred celebration of friendship, on 1 May, as well as various other meals throughout the course of the year, depending on how much money is raised. The names of these clubs are very similar to those of the old academies. And they are truly the academies of the common folk, far more substantial and lively and friendly than literary academies, where members eat, play music, sing, declaim, joke and play pranks, improvise, play drinking games, enjoy feelings of fraternal camaraderie and, ultimately, let time go by, simply and peacefully.

In the common society of Rome, democratic, free, adult, and devoid of complexes, there is room for everyone, for every human condition and type. There are plenty of strange people, unthinkable apparitions: immense men, who carry their outsized bodies with casual confidence, women dressed in the clothing of fifty years ago, creatures from distant and forgotten times and places. A man may appear dressed from head to foot in ivy leaves, living proof of the deep-rooted passion for the republic; and at the Hotel Biscione you may see an elderly gentleman whose claim to fame is that he is the spitting image of the late King Victor Emmanuel III. Herders of cattle, goats, and sheep all live at Villa Doria, in the heart of the city, in huts made of leafy branches, just as they do in the forests of the Sila, keeping alive all the old pastoral customs. A motley crew packs into the Totocalcio football betting shops every Saturday night, to place the last bets before the match on Sunday: The profoundly deaf, who gesticulate in animated discussions of odds and hopes, beggars, old women, priests, and tram conductors who have just finished their last run of the evening. In the street, you may happen upon solitary musicians playing antiquated instruments, in empty lanes where the sound echoes as if in a seashell, or drunks who speak seriously as they confide their views of Science, the World, and Destiny. I met a taxi driver one evening when I was out walking my dog Baruc; he began playing with the dog and then finally walked me all the way home, telling me that dogs are angels, with citations from Baudelaire, Leopardi, and Bakunin, all of whom loved animals. When we reached my front door, he shook my hand and said, 'I am an anarchist. Tonight I am happy, because I have seen you and this dog. I am completely happy: I wish that I could kiss this dog...and kill a man.'

Each of these characters, in the great forest of Rome, is intrinsic, perfect, and complete unto themselves, perfectly achieved. Their poetry cannot be operatic or novelistic. It is perforce epic (the thousands of sonnets written by Belli from a single epic poem). But who could ever describe them all? Behind every window, in the continuous movement of the architecture, of the yellow and violet walls, there is a unique, real person, fully realized, waiting only to be seen, to be revealed. Who could ever catalogue all these living, self-confident truths? The women, the young beauties in the marketplaces and the windows, the old women sitting on doorsteps, and the children, too, in their incessantly mobile childish life, in a certain sense already adult? What I can say about them here is nothing more than a fleeting hint, a flash in an infinite stream.

The personality of the Roman people changes according to the differences in place; and what I have tried to describe, admittedly only a tiny facet of the whole, is the people of the quarters of ancient Rome, where that people has lived since time out of mind, at one with stone and memory. But, increasingly distant from that lovely city centre, there lives another people, hailing from every part of Italy. In the monstrous modern working-class quarters, beyond the Porta San Giovanni or the Piazza Bologna or at the far end of the Via Nomentana, in the nameless beehives built in keeping with the architectural sadism of the years of the Fascist regime in Italy, the people itself loses its character, its confidence, its style, the contact and resemblance with its homes, dwindling away into a featureless and ever poorer underclass. All the way out of the poverty of the great belt surrounding Rome, the rats of the Garbatella, to the dew ponds of Primavalle, to the villages of hovels, the shanty towns, the grottoes of the Viale Tiziano and the Viale degli Acquedotti. This too is Rome, but it is no longer inhabited by the ancient people, straightforward and proud and noble and openly sceptical of the artisans and traders, but a proletariat in formation, with varied dark passions, or a mob of paupers, struggling against hunger, loneliness, and complete destitution. This too is Rome, even if it seems to be part of another world. And if I have limited myself here to the age-old people of Rome, one cannot exist without the other, into which it continually plunges or from which it rises. In my book *The Watch* I tried to describe them both, and the synchronicity and the juxtaposition of times and individual destinies in the great forest of Rome. I wrote about Teresa, the cigarette seller, the things that Giacinto, the waiter, would say, and Elena, the one-legged prostitute, and Rosa, the Jewess of the Garbatella, and the newspaper typesetters, and the dark hellish world of rented rooms, and the wandering musicians, Fortunato and the blind man, and beggars, and the *luigini*,* the ministries, politicians, idlers, women, priests, children, and the thousand other persons and moments of Rome's eternal present.

The roaring of lions in the night
Of the depths of time to memory
Owls, madonnas, symbols, interrupted
Events, timeless, outside of history

Thickets of houses, birds, branches, caverns,
Courtyards of rats and fallen glory,
And eyes and voices, and gestures, and gold, and slag
The green return of corrupted ages,

Brigands in the forest, serpents at the breast,
Real kings and false, ministries and beggars,
Peasants at the plough and worms in the saddle,

Ancient lament and funeral eulogy,
Courage, and hunger, and patient men,
And Rome, and Italy: this is the Watch.[4]

That is what I wrote, in the sonnet that serves as an opening epigram for this book, and for what I think of as Rome and the infinite and infinitely individual life that flows there like an unbroken river.

* [*Translator's note.* A term coined by Levi to denote a political lackey who inflicts cruel treatment on the poor and weak, while fawning upon the wealthy and powerful. It originated with the character of the Fascist mayor of Gagliano, Don Luigino Magalone, who featured in his book *Cristo si è fermato a Eboli* (1945; *Christ Stopped at Eboli*). The term *luigino* (plural *luigini*) appears in several of Levi's books.]

But this too is nothing, in the face of the manifold reality. The elderly common folk of Rome, who bear and who are aware of this elusive infinity, have derived from it, over the generations, a simple life, a few simple truths. And, as the fishmonger of Campo dei Fiori put it, 'after the truth, there's nothing more to say.'

* * *

This secular space rejects all descriptions that aspire to depict it as whole and entire, since, with the development and evolution of its architecture, rather than existing in a single place (which is the same place as always, stratified, excavated, pounded by the echo of countless footsteps), it extends throughout time and, like time, it both exists and doesn't exist simultaneously, shifting and immobile, stable and fleeting, ephemeral and eternal. Each of these meanings can be taken as the only true version and all of them exist together, like the facets of a crystal, simultaneously. This is not lost, is never lost, and need not be sought after, because it is apparent and open in its crannies of stone and yet cannot be wholly identified with any of them, while in its permanence it shifts as rapidly as the beat of the heart, or the flicker of the eyelash. And so, they have all portrayed Rome or described it as their heart dictated (without the naive Cubist claim to totality, which juxtaposes all possible identities) and have found in that paradigm of present history a moment of their own life. The name of Rome, the most mythological of all the goddess cities, this name that in its original form, Roma, is the reverse of Amor, its mirror image, must necessarily mirror itself, in order to exist, in a specific moment or in a specific being, in a relationship, in one of the myriad relationships of love. 'A world are you, O Rome, but without love/the world is not the world

In the common society of Rome, democratic, free, adult, and devoid of complexes, there is room for everyone, for every human condition and type.

and neither can Rome be Rome.'[5] Rome then lives in its mirror and changes with it, according to an infinite array of angles of refraction: the contradictory there is equally true. And so Rome, depending on the various voices, speaks all languages. It still speaks Latin, both the Latin of the ancient Romans and the Latin of the church, it speaks bureaucratic Italian and literary Italian, and it still speaks its own language, the *romanesco* dialect spoken by Belli, through the mouths of the common people, and the patois of the *borgate*, or the grim quarters of the periphery, the almost aphasic attempt at self-expression of a world still locked in the darkness of non-existence.[6] Everyone has found in it precisely what they are: images of emotions, of all the love and hate, all the happiness and grief and boredom and vitality and apathy imaginable. As if in some symbolic convergence, the ancient vexed question of Italy and the Italians continued to waver in the ambiguous relationship with Rome, the ambiguous impulse that variously attracts or repels, causing the city to be considered, variously, angelic or diabolical. In the language of symbols or institutions and historical ideologies, Rome may appear as an indispensable centre of life or the enemy of all reality, and 'those people in Rome' are still, in the mouth of the peasant, people from another world, unsympathetic and hostile. Rome, or death: it was true, just as it is true that for many, for 'l'uva puttanella dei piccoli',[7] Rome is death. In individual mirrors, Rome rediscovers all the forms and all the aspects of the soul. 'I have Rome and happiness,'[8] sang Umberto Saba at a certain point, after the dark years of servitude and war. 'But for Deda it was axiomatic that we should not go to Rome.' (It was true, too, for Mario Soldati, who, after having lived there, decided to flee back to the air of his northern birthplace, far from that fatal centre of church and corruption.)[9]

[A][I saw it, too, like everyone, [writes C. L. many years later][10] with different eyes, depending on my own internal time, different if I was arriving there as a young man,[11] or if I lived there, imprisoned,[12] or if I returned there in happy and in tragic times,[13] when time seemed to stand still in order to set free a boundless vitality, full of the hope and the joy of pure existence. The Rome of that time truly was *The Watch*.[14] It was the glittering eyes of Teresa, who sold cigarettes on the street corner. This 'Open City'[15] opened itself up to all the countless new destinies that lived, concealed in the sleep of reality]: [C][then, like a seashell slowly clamping shut at the surge of water that signals the approach of some nameless danger, it appeared, little by little, to retreat into its own life, into the pattern of its daily life and its political and bureaucratic functions, and their new forms which, in various ways, simply mirrored the old ones,] [B][when that profound and general vitality seemed to reduce itself to the arrogant and physical vitality of a youth as brilliant as the pitiless sun burning high in the sky]; [D][another chapter of that history was being written when the ideals seemed to collapse and the boredom of the petty bourgeoisie described by Moravia[16] took the place of the happiness hailed by Saba, and it seemed necessary to seek out a sombre, fragile relic of that happiness in the most atrocious sites of despair, in the patois and the gestures of something close to non-existence, something close to nothingness, in the protest of the 'not yet' against an organized nothing].[17]

This too, however, is a passing period of history, already waning and changing before our eyes, upon the great body of Rome. Only the focus of attention can have altered neighbourhoods and streets, as if in a poetic regulatory plan that drives development in one area or another and, from moment to moment, illuminates the palaces of the nobility, the churches, the streets of the middle class, or the hovels of the poor. Everything changes at the speed of time, in the motionless time of Rome. Fifteen burdensome years of counter-reformation seem to have brought us back to the sense of living for the day, the fleeting hour, the sense of death that can be found in the poetry of seventeenth-century Rome, when Góngora wrote: 'Oh Roma, en tu grandeza y tu hermosura/huyó lo que era firme, y solamente/lo fugitivo permanece y dura.'[18]

The 'fleeting moment' of Rome in these years is the external and evident history of the Italian ruling class, the fragile immobility of a restoration, the apathetic succession of scandals, speculations, deals, enrichments, the apparent triumph of a clerical bourgeoisie and, flowing through the ruins, much like the river that so deeply moved the Spanish poet, is a glittering river of cars pounding the ancient roadways. The problems have been given other names: they have become the general problems of our country. Rome has increasingly become a capital city and the ancient traditional indifference of its people, which is taken for granted and discussed continually, is more of a recurrence of history, an attitude, a hue, than a reality. It has been said so many times that Rome is a tomb, a magnificent classical tomb in which the hopes of Italy have been laid piously to rest; but when, in July 1960, the burden of an unrepresentative regime seemed for an instant intolerable, the common folk of Rome, old and young, rose up and fought at Porta San Paolo.[19] No longer a tomb, that day: something quite alive, filled with hidden strength.

'Rome is a bomb,' I wrote back then.[20] Dark and deep, they are afraid of it; they have long been afraid of it – but they don't know that, or they have forgotten it – they want to remain deaf and blind. Slumbering in their eternal lassitude, in the massive sleepiness of digestion, in the resurgent barbarism that daily destroys the landmarks of history, in the deals that are so easy that to them they seem matters of course that will never run out, here they are, encamped like ancient enemies who will never fit in. Too many years as the capital of pre-Fascism and Fascism and post-Fascism and neo-Fascism,[21] but always Fascism in various guises, has made them into the very image of Rome that is most detested by peasants. 'Those people in Rome' hold the keys, all the keys, the keys of silver and gold, the keys to the land and even the keys to the hereafter, the keys to the world, all the riches of earth, as well as disdain, the look that doesn't see.

Here, more than anywhere else in Italy, two worlds coexist and confront each other, distinct and separate: the powerful and the people. And the powerful are the most powerful, shameless, to such a degree that they have stopped worrying about appearance, so cunning that they can abandon the use of cunning, to the point that they allow themselves to be symbolized without disguise in their *cioccetti*,* increasingly closed off and isolated, and scorned, and generally and diffusely corrupt. In them, we seem to see an omnium gatherum of the ancient evils of Italy, the age-old weakness and violence, the heritage of feudalism and paternalism, the ritualism and idolatry, the defilement of things, whether sacred or not: and the pessimism with a vested interest and a double standard, the chilly cynicism that believes man is corrupt in his very nature (and can find salvation only in a good death).

On the opposing side is one of the most alive, and unaffected, and humanely adult peoples on earth: simple, ancient; with all the variety of a city that is of the people rather than proletarian, where all the ages have unfolded and endure, present. And its profound culture made up of the works of the centuries and of the men of today; its great surrounding belt of poverty, with the ordeals and the fears of every hour and every day, and the expectation of the right to live, to work, to be citizens, to enter, physically, through the gates, and still ready, in their ways, to find within themselves,

* [*Translator's note.* A reference to Urbano Cioccetti, mayor of Rome from 1958 to 1961.]

life and liberty. It is a people, in its various strata, when the time is right, that possesses maturity, unity, solidarity, and generosity. In October 1922, at San Lorenzo shots were fired.[22] At Porta San Paolo, on 8 September 1943, the Italian Resistance began. At Porta San Paolo, on 6 July 1960 the New Italian Resistance made itself heard. They were all there, members of every layer of the populace, by natural instinct, without calculation or hesitation or qualms, there to defend the state that they themselves personify, that must be present in things. And leading the charge were the young, filled with an active, self-aware clarity, filled with bravery. These shining young people made up for the grim weight of the Fascist and clerical sirocco, much like those young partisans in Florence who, in 1944, inspired and consoled the poet: 'But I saw the noble blood of your young men and women flow red in the street, purifying your soul once again.'[23]

That this capacity for renewal and purification should take as its representative and creator, in the most extraordinary moments, the common folk of Rome, may seem miraculous and almost incredible: because this people has appeared to one and all immobile over the centuries, unchanging and complete in its narrow scope of life, whatever the variations of the stars. Conflagrations, formulas, false ideals, political jargon, all leave it unmoved. For this people to move, to be moved, as we have all seen with our own eyes, requires something very simple and real, which can touch a fundamental aspect of its nature. And what could that ever be?

CHAPTER II

The Solitude of Rome

Even if you never leave your home, stay shut up in your room, never look out of the window, never read the newspaper, and never talk with the caretaker, even a recluse, a convict, a monk, or an invalid, even the blind, in Rome, cannot help but notice festivals. You can't help but notice, because the very air around you, the feel of it, its consistency, its elasticity, its basic nature, seems to have changed. There are tiny, almost undetectable signs, but, from early morning, you can feel something trembling; above all you can hear a difference in the usual sequence of sounds; that continuous hum, like a seashell placed against the ear, which is the baroque sound of the city, instead, reaches the ear somehow altered, broken here and there, riddled with unexpected cracklings and abrupt silences. Indeed, we might say that festivals, at least the major festivals, in Rome, are resonant and atmospheric and are celebrated by noise and in the air. They are, in the final analysis, country festivals and so, suddenly, and all at once, the city returns to what it was before the dawn of history: countryside and forest; and the machine-made sounds of the city give way to the cries of animals and the rustling of leaves.

On religious feast days, the air is altered by the thrumming, near and far, of bells, the mutterings of enormous animals lying in wait, the humming of gilded insects perched on the branches and flowers of the city's architecture. On the last of the year, long before midnight is rocked with explosions, the whole day echoes with joyful alarms: these are warning shots, like rifles accidentally fired by hunters in the urban forest. But there are just two major festivals, two real festivals, festivals that have nothing to do with those of other cities or other nations, or which, even if shared with other countries, still reflect the age-old agrarian nature of this city – a city of shepherds buried beneath a city of soldiers, in turn buried beneath a city of lawyers, buried beneath a city of priests, buried beneath a city of artisans and shopkeepers, buried beneath a city of bureaucrats, buried, in its turn, under who can say what other city – and these two festivals are San Giovanni, or the feast of St John, and the *Befana*, or Epiphany, in the Piazza Navona.

The feast of St John has lost, in part, its more archaic and wondrous aspects; I still remember them, having seen them many times prior to 1930. Then, much more than now, it was a mad pagan festivity honouring a prophetically baroque animal: the snail. Millions and millions of snails were sacrificed in the honoured presence of the saint on the altars of neighbourhood restaurants; it seemed that the snail's slightly slimy flavour of earth and forest helped the Romans to revert to earthy forest animals. Falling enthusiastic prey to a sacred rapture, these sylvan creatures crowded the piazza by the light of Catherine wheels and other fireworks, brandishing sacred garlic plants like so many clubs and flailing orgiastically with these garlic plants at the heads and shoulders of their fellow participants in this summer ceremony. They were taken over, at some point, by the bureaucratic 'leisure-time' organizations and the virtuosity of the police: beneath the conformist umbrella of organized celebrations, the free-form frenzy of the summer solstice subsided and, though it never vanished entirely, it lost much of its magical ferocity; it dwindled and thinned.

The celebration of the winter solstice, on the other hand, survived intact. Although Twelfth Night, dedicated to children, witches, the Magi, apparitions, the spirit world, and the star of Bethlehem, was also laid siege by the wily advocates of virtue and order, it managed to fend off the attacks. This year, brooms were outlawed. By ancient custom brooms were wielded as weapons, not only to ward off evil spirits, or to ensure the benevolence of hags and witches, but also, much as garlic plants in summer, to beat the heads and shoulders of those taking part in the ritual. The prohibition against brooms extended to those obnoxious rag balls tied to an elastic cord, launched as treacherous, invisible projectiles. I must say that, for once, the intervention of the authorities – which, in instances of this sort, and in many other instances, tends to be unfortunate and wrong-headed – actually did some good; while preserving the unrefined and spontaneous nature of this festival, it freed it of the pranksters who had spoiled its original charm.

Even if you never leave your home, stay shut up in your room, never look out of the window, never read the newspaper, and never talk with the caretaker, even a recluse, a convict, a monk, or an invalid, even the blind, in Rome, cannot help but notice festivals.

From afar, you can sense a sort of throbbing and shrilling in the air, and that alone begins to tug you towards a different world. The closer you come to the Piazza Navona, the greater this throbbing becomes, growing, little by little, into a vague, thundering din, a continual chant, a chorus of countless sounds; and, as if by some absurd piece of magic, as you are swept into the crowd, it seems as if there is a rushing river in the broad lake of the piazza, the buildings, the churches, and the palaces all seem to vanish, and where a city once stood there is now nothing but a vast, primitive meadowland populated in the night by millions of crickets, all chirping together, in unison, in the looming shadow of the fields, beneath a black night sky.

Everyone has a whistle and everyone is blowing into their own, trying to drown out the others. There are whistles of every sort, from simple tin whistles to plastic whistles; from long, two-barrelled whistles to more complicated ones, which make the sound of a football referee's whistle, or the sound of a train's or ship's horn, or whistles shaped like animals, hens, or cocks, covered with colourful feathers. There they stand, whistling, in the piazza, in their tens of thousands. That's all there is to the festive celebration: disarming in its simplicity. But this collective whistle alone is enough to transform Rome into the archaic countryside, deserted and solitary.

I bought myself a whistle, too, and, just for fun, I started to blow on it. Progressively, that childish and age-old enthusiasm, which I could see everyone else sharing, began to grow within me as well, and my whistle joined with the sound of all the countless other crickets in the Piazza Navona. And as my whistle grew louder, stronger, and more determined, I realized that the sound issuing from my little instrument was enveloping me like a compact atmosphere and that in this sonorous atmosphere, as if within an invisible suit of armour, I grew more and more to be part of the crowd surrounding me; and yet at the same time, I was increasingly isolated from it, until, in the heart of that fully attained communion, I had also reached a state of perfect solitude. As I looked at the faces of those around me, I saw in each the same happiness: the happiness of complete solitude amidst an immense crowd. Perhaps this explains the great popularity of the deafening little engines of the Vespa and the Lambretta that create a transparent but impenetrable wall of sound, transporting us out into the world while isolating us from it.

United like some great swarm beneath this cupola of sound and separated one from another by a personal resonating diaphragm, like the wax walls of the cells in a beehive, the crowd flowed around the stalls of toys and candyfloss, and the magnificent shooting galleries. It considered itself as reflected in others: happy to be alive today, on this clear winter evening, and to be alive together, through the artifice of an immeasurable sound, on an endless, motionless summer night, long before cities and events, in an unchanging archaic countryside, in the dark immobile primitive solitude of the soul.

CHAPTER III

The Two-Cent Coin

I don't go out much during the day; I try to preserve the time I have for work. The streets are full of charms and opportunities. Simple and everyday encounters and appearances conceal enchanted worlds from which the hapless stroller, having once ventured in, cannot turn back, held spellbound by the strongest sense of all, the greedy and truthful eye, more powerful even than an iron will, in a land of metamorphosis and synchronicity. 'In the sinuous folds of ancient capitals'[1] (if I may be permitted so barbarously literal a translation) you can find anything you want, all of the aspects of grandeur and squalor, the real and the fanciful, all of the overlaid and finite planes of time: living people and their sounds, the survivors, the architecture shaped eloquently by the passing years, the changing fashions, the cars, the animals, and the countless manifestations of an endless world.

I was walking, one of these evenings, down an empty street, behind the majestic Palazzo Borghese. A nightwatchman, who had leant his bicycle against the wall of a house, called to me from a distance to hurry, if I didn't want to miss a rare spectacle. In the gloomy corner of a closed portal stood a large rat, being assailed by five cats. It stood motionless in the darkness, shrilling fiercely like a tiny brute, while the cats – those large stray cats, veterans, like knights of old or soldiers of fortune, of a thousand battles in the ruins of the Forum, with glorious and threadbare scars of long-ago duels, as ferocious as German students – those five cats of war, were afraid. They crept near, ready to pounce, but as the rat screeched, they retreated; one by one, they turned tail and disappeared down the alley, amidst scrap paper and refuse. Just one cat, striped like a tiger, the most obstinate of the lot, held its ground. It ventured an attack, but the rat squeaked and readied a counterassault, halting the cat midway. The rat stared back, squealing, motionless in its corner, like a hero out of Leopardi. Then, suddenly, it moved, in no hurry, turning every so often with a shrill squeak to face down the cat that followed it, and covered two or three metres of open ground along the wall (an immense distance, comparable to what a soldier, venturing out of a trench and across a clearing swept by machine-gun fire, must cover, trusting his soul to the Lord above), and then vanished in a flash, down the mouth of a sewer. The night-watchman, in his black uniform and shiny boots, was delighted by the show. He would have stayed there for hours, entirely unmindful of the doors that needed to be checked and marked as such with a ticket, enraptured by that animal epic.

I walked on a little further, past the cobblestones of the Via dell'Arancio. There I saw a sign advertising an 'Exhibition of Paintings by the Traffic Police'. How do the traffic police see the world? There they stand, in the middle of crossroads, on the street, in marketplaces, everywhere; they must keep order amidst the chaotic city that surrounds them and assails them from every direction, they must transform that fluid, incandescent material into articles of regulations, by-laws, codes, and acts. What might they see through those rules; how can they stop for a moment to appreciate and take part in that amorphous movement, motionless as they must remain?

It wasn't the right time to go to see a show. Not far away, at the end of the bridge, I found two policemen directing traffic. They were big, strapping, dark men wearing new uniforms. Whenever I talk to policemen, I cannot help but remember my earliest childhood impression of how big they are, how questionable their humanity. As a little boy, I was walking alone in the street for the first time, on my way to Rayneri Primary School, when I found a two-cent coin on the pavement. Children's eyes, so close to the ground, see so many things! I stooped to pick up the coin, but it burned in my hand like stolen treasure. I ran as fast as I could until I reached the policeman who stood on the corner of the Corso Valentino and, in a tempest of conflicting, glorious passions, I delivered the coin to him, so that he could restore it to its rightful owner. He was a policeman as massive as a tower and I peered up at him from my vantage point, expecting something magnificent from his godlike power, praise or perhaps reproof. But the policeman took the coin and burst out laughing. This was my first glimpse of the irrational humanity of power.

The streets are full of charms and opportunities. Simple and everyday encounters and appearances conceal enchanted worlds

I asked the two policemen at the bridge when I could see the show. They were delighted. 'There are some beautiful paintings,' they said. 'Obviously you are an artist yourself.' They weren't sure if it was open in the afternoon, and they told me to ring the City of Rome, by dialling 661, to find out. I did ring but, because the telephones in Rome are like so many sieves allowing the voices that surge along the lines to leak out in all directions, when I enquired about the hours of the traffic policemen's exhibition, the response was: 'This is the Italian parliament, and painting is of no concern to us.' I had been put through to 660, a number where no one is interested in art. It's a good thing, I thought to myself, that it wasn't 666, where no one is interested in anything at all, because that is the number of the Antichrist.

The traffic policemen's paintings are lovely, almost too lovely. Many of them are true artists. They know their art; one worked in the style of Rosai, another in the style of Bartolini, and there were many other references. Others still were ordinary 'Sunday painters', with the untutored grace that is so typical of them. For them, painting is – as it is for all dilettantes, whatever their normal occupation, be they heads of state, like Churchill or Eisenhower, or doctors, professionals, factory workers (only peasants never seem to paint in this style) – a pastime, a fanciful form of relaxation. But there is something specific and common to the traffic policemen's paintings and it emerges, naturally enough, in the less painterly canvases. Perhaps it is a quest for, and an idealization of, themselves as ordinary men, apart from their role as enforcers of rules and order, in an imaginary world in which there is no need for rules and order. In all of their paintings of houses and streets and cities, there is never a single passer-by, not a single human figure, not a car, not a child, not an animal: ideal deserted streets, without traffic lights, without traffic, without noise, so many paradises of solitude. Even the shanty towns on the outskirts of Rome are empty, deserted in the bright sunlight. The needy, poverty-stricken inhabitants, in such flagrant violation of the city code, have vanished. A policeman need not keep order or issue fines, and he can paint in blessed peace. When a policeman paints or sculpts himself, he portrays himself modestly, small, skinny, with a melancholy, human face, his arms filled with Christmas gifts. And the still lifes are homely ones: a carafe, a coffee grinder. One canvas is entitled 'Article 11' (the article of law that prohibits hanging out the washing to dry over city streets), and it depicts a street in the old part of Rome, narrow and shadowy, with sheets and shirts festooning the peeling walls and the tottering architecture. Here, too, no one walks down these streets, no one draped those sheets over those lines, there is no one to fine, and the washing itself – in violation of every rule – is seen with the loving and disinterested eye of the painter. By painting in this way, these divine regulators of the urban jungle, these giant representatives of authority and municipal power, are still human enough to laugh at the sight of a child, presenting with shy pride – on a long-forgotten morning – a two-cent coin.

CHAPTER IV

Sunday Stroll

I step out into the boulevards of the Villa Borghese, outside the water garden and the dog shows, where the animals laze in boredom, imprisoned in their cages, while the ladies who own them weep the real tears of children at the prizes they failed to secure. Springtime gleams in its Sunday best, bursting with fresh sap and tender greens, slightly powdered with the faintest grey veil of dust, beneath a sky puffed out like a skirt tossing in the breeze. People are already lying on the lawns, as if it were summer. Forgetful of his meagre trade, a seller of *lupini* beans sleeps on the grass, his hat pulled down over his eyes; beside him sit his wooden tub and his packets of beans, wrapped in yellow paper; girls stroll in pairs, hand in hand. Mirrored in the lake sits a little boat, beneath the columns of the neoclassical temple; not far away a few of the skinny Egyptian lions that inhabit this city, which abounds with a rich and variegated fauna of stone, spit water with the nonchalant bonhomie of poets.[1] The clock, the famous water clock of the Pincio, marks the eternal hours of Sunday, its paddles moving slowly within its artificial plant-like structure, and the donkey cart, lying empty, waiting for its triumphant young passengers, the name 'Coca-Cola' glistening across its red-painted sides.

Just now, the children have no time to ride in the donkey cart; they stand, arranged carefully by height, smallest to tallest in rows, staring at the little puppet theatre. There is Pulcinella, or Punch, with his nasal voice and his incomprehensible jargon (the children, though, understand him). I stop, ready to enjoy, yet again, the enchantment, never-changing, that still draws me in – who can say with what illusions – and has done so ever since my father first revealed to us, when we had barely learned to talk, the ancient laws of the theatre, skilfully moving the fingers that he had slipped into the head and arms of puppets. The show had begun some time before and was coming to an end. But what was this peculiar puppet show? Pulcinella wanted to serenade an invisible girl named Gabriella. Suddenly, unseen, out sneaked a devil, dressed all in red, his bald head red, armed with his inevitable cudgel and raining blows on Pulcinella's head, the inevitable cudgel blows that for whatever reason seem to move us to laughter. This improbable devil would disappear each time that Pulcinella, whining and sobbing, whirled around and there seemed to be no reasonable explanation for him, save as some sort of conscience, stinging and reproaching Pulcinella for whatever unnamed sin he may have committed.

Finally Pulcinella saw the devil and managed to wrestle the cudgel away from him. But, once he was armed with that age-old weapon, he was completely unable to pay him back in kind: the devil is elusive by his very nature and at last managed to recover his club and bring it down, once and for all, on poor Pulcinella's head. As Pulcinella stood weeping, before him there appeared the maiden Gabriella, whose face seemed Chinese but whose voice was that of an ogre, and together they danced, driving away all care. Then Pulcinella tried to give her a kiss, whereupon the girl vanished and in her place stood Death himself, with his round white skull. Pulcinella turned away, trembling in terror: now the girl returned, ready for a kiss, while Pulcinella retreated in fear, certain that she was actually Death. At last, she persuaded him to turn around and, behold, she really was Death again and he was kissing Death instead of the girl. This scene was replayed, once, twice, and a third time, until finally Pulcinella collapsed in a corner, overwhelmed by horror, and the curtain came down.

Even the children seemed a little frightened. They, who always know by heart every line and every move of this their own theatre and who defend every aspect against change, were bemused by this story of devils, death, and perhaps psychoanalysis, resembling a scene from the Mexican 'Day of the Dead' ritual. Or perhaps, in the happy dreamy Sunday atmosphere, this was nothing but a reminiscence of the baroque era and the Counter-Reformation, an image from Belli, dropped artfully before its proper audience: nannies, soldiers, and children.

Forgetful of his meagre trade, a seller of lupini beans sleeps on the grass, his hat pulled down over his eyes

That men, whether living or dead,
Have a death's head inside their own head.[2]

What sort of death's head the American woman at the counter of the cafe concealed in her beautifully groomed head, a few steps further along, was not easy to say. It was hard to say how old she might be, somewhere between fifty, perhaps, and seventy, exceedingly elegant, made-up, clearly an adept of massages, beauty treatments, creams, and science. Her hair was dyed white, with the slightest haze of light blue; her unwrinkled face was daubed girlishly in pink, her tiny hands emerged from long, well-made black suede gloves, her petite feet were enclosed in exceedingly soft slippers adorned with a silk bow, her black silk outfit was studded with ornaments and decorated with frills, at once sober and fanciful. She was an elegant 'sophisticate' from Park Avenue, and at that time of day she wore her drunkenness with confident stylishness. She spoke English to the barman, and he answered in the same language. She was drinking a negroni.

'Can I take a bottle of negroni *originale* back with me to America?'

'Of course.'

'How do you make it?'

'One part bitters, one part Carpano, and the rest gin.'

'No, no gin.'

'Without gin, it's not a negroni; it's something else.'

'But I want a negroni *originale* without gin.'

With her negroni she was eating buttered canapés with caviar and salmon.

'Why are they buttered?'

'That's how we make them here: they are buttered canapés.'

'Couldn't I have them without butter?'

'Sure, but then they would be something different. The Italians like their canapés buttered.'

'Couldn't I have Rome without Italians?'

Negroni without gin, canapés without butter, Rome without Italians, this scene out of Hemingway[3] went on and on, starting all over again for pages and pages: Rome, the canapés, the negronis, the negronis, the canapés and Rome, and so on. There were no bulls, no bullfighters awaiting us. Only, if I had chosen, the canvases of the so-called 'Giovane pittura'[4] (*giovane* referring to the youthful ages of the artists themselves) in Valle Giulia, where I was now walking, just as arid, elegant, and empty as the youthful soul of the elderly American woman.

CHAPTER V

The Helicopter

Within a soap bubble that a child releases into the air and then tracks with an enchanted gaze as it floats away, within the transparent sphere of an insect's eye, the eye of a giant cobbled-together dragonfly buzzing over a hedge, enclosed in a hollow glass retort like a homunculus in a story about an alchemist, we float off the earth and rise, as if by imaginary levitation, straight up into the sky.

It is a Roman Sunday full of rapidly shifting clouds and sudden gusts of wind. A few drops of rain had fallen, earlier, as if threatening a shower, but the sun re-emerged from behind the glowing bank of clouds and shone down on the grassy fields, now and then wreathed in mist, beaming and waning over and over like a warm luminous pulse. The transparent bubble in which we are enclosed focuses the sunlight like some odd incubator packed with cranks, handles, pedals, reminiscent of the old-fashioned bicycles of my childhood. For many years, as a boy, I dreamt that I could hover this way, like a bird, by merely moving my arms, and that I could move in mid-air from house to house, past windows, weightless, drifting freely in any direction, gazing down upon the world below, unbound by the grim burden of gravity, as I passed overhead separate, lofty, unhindered, spanning all distances. I was in a dimension without boundaries or chains, which was perhaps the sphere of absolute indeterminate power, where everything is as possible as it is unreal. (Was I dreaming or imagining? For if it was a dream, it was so vivid and persuasive that it seemed quite real, and deep down I was sure that I really did possess these dream powers.) This dream, or this symbolic imagining of my youth, came to mind as the earth, held down by its weight, sank beneath us as we wheeled wingless in the colourful air.

Even the helicopter's very shape, at once so weird, natural, and archaic, like a living prehistoric machine, gives free rein to the imagination. Both the name, which could easily describe a family of insects, and the drone of the spinning blades, identical to the sound of rapidly whirring sheath wings, call to mind the mechanical animal universe of bushes, stamens, and pistils and of nuptial flights. Next to me, the pilot, with his earphones for radio communications, his hands enclosed in old scuffed leather gloves, appears as a living contradiction of the law of gravity. He is a fat man, rotund, weighty, immense, with the serious, good-natured face of mechanics and navigators, his massive body barely fitting into his tight, short flying suit. He is an expert helicopter pilot, a military pilot well trained in these three-dimensional voyages, accustomed to setting his craft down delicately in the tightest, most inaccessible places, summoned by the urgent necessities of a rescue, a delivery, a presence that would otherwise be impossible. Shouting over the engine's roar and communicating with our hands, we set our course, and already we are far away, flying over the furthest houses of Rome.

Flying in a helicopter is different from flying in an aeroplane. Aeroplanes are all about speed, distance, transport, running in a straight line, bringing the four corners of the world ever closer, eliminating objects and shrinking the dimensions of time, lengthening or shrinking the hours, depending on whether you are flying with the sun or against it. Flying in a helicopter is really all about flying: it takes place in space, not time. It looms, close in, over real things, with the added sense of lightness, the power of detachment; from its spherical and transparent eye, it offers everything to one's vision.

Now, Rome lies spread out at our feet. All around us it opens out in all its countless aspects, in the tiny details that seem so close, as recognizable as if we were looking down with the sharp eyes of a giant, a curious Gulliver on the island of Lilliput. And the passage of people, the scurrying of pedestrians, the flow of car traffic, the countless little events, all now seen to be occurring simultaneously, take on a Lilliputian strangeness viewed from the vantage point of a giant. Right now, the stadium lies below us. The football teams Roma and Sampdoria are playing a match and it looks (at least from here) like an exciting game. We hover motionless for a few minutes to watch, and we recognize, tiny and distinct in their red jerseys, players that the Sunday crowds know and love, stepping like so many brightly coloured insects, geometric motions on the green surface of the playing field. The spectators, their heads swathed in yellow, turn their eyes upwards to take in the apparition hovering above them and then immediately return their gaze to the fascinating motions of the ball. Then we leap upwards and we are immediately further along, heading back towards the Via Cassia over the new blocks of flats in Vigna Clara. On a terrace, I recognize a friend who waves at me, his handkerchief fluttering in the wind,[1] while his wife raises both arms and their children, frightened by this deafening butterfly, weep in fear. Another leap into the transparent air and we are over the secret gardens of the Pope, over the buildings of the Vatican. We orbit the dome of St Peter's, magnificently intersecting (and it is even clearer, up here, from this new dimension, than from below) with the exedra of the columns in the great piazza. The faithful, clustering around the obelisk, stare up at us in astonishment, as if an absurd mechanical dove, heralding inconceivable events, had appeared in the sacred air above the basilica.

And now all of Rome discloses to me its hidden world of rooftops and terraces. It is in the hidden niches of windows, with whole families lazing on terraces, like flocks of sheep in meadows; in the infinite variety of shapes in ancient quarters where the wonders of the architect's imagination display their unknown side, the covers of those purple-and-gold coffers that house all the ages of history. And the modern neighbourhoods, gigantic, glittering, and greedy like arrays of gears or cogs, and the ruins of the Forum, the remains of the bombardment of time. And the parks, swollen with leafy branches and the life of plants. And there, not far from the palaces and monuments and aqueducts, the hovels of the poor, the belt that runs around Rome like a temporary campsite of tribes, biding their time in those shanties until the day comes when they can enter the city. We fly over and around my old home overlooking Piazza del Gesù. I identify the window from which, for so many years, I used to look out on the world, watching as the black swallows flew, leaving trails, across the broad twilit sky. Like a swallow I dart past that window, wishing that I could fly in and swoop down to the fountain in the courtyard, but the electric wires bar my way. The Quirinal flies its flag proudly, we run along the 'Manica Lunga'[2] (and it really is long, very long indeed) and then we are over the stairway of the Trinità dei Monti, gleaming white among the golden buildings around it, designed as a sharp-edged, perfect baroque balcony. The trees of the Villa Strohl-Fern, where I live now, crowded with blackbirds and squirrels, are remarkably dense and compact (could we land in my own back garden?). We turn on the axis of our rotor and head back into old Rome, practically grazing the top of the Porta del Popolo, looking up the three streets that, like three dark, straight canals, flow into the open

Now, Rome lies spread out at our feet. All around us it opens out in all its countless aspects, in the tiny details that seem so close, as recognizable as if we were looking down with the sharp eyes of a giant, a curious Gulliver on the island of Lilliput.

basin of the piazza. We rush along the entire length of the Corso like ancient barbarians and, a moment later, we are at St John Lateran and over the Via Appia. We descend upon the houses of friends and acquaintances, to pay visits, like demigods and then, flying just over the countryside (we could, you might say, count the infinite blades of grass, number one by one the flowers of the field),[3] we turn towards the sea. We fly hugging the ground, hopping over obstacles, houses, electric wires, zipping lightly over depressions and ravines, almost grazing hilltops, practically touching the fleeces of the sheep that flee madly in all directions while white dogs gallop along after us, barking fiercely at the whirlybird, already long gone. And then we are over the Sunday beaches, following the white hem of waves edging a transparent sea. In the empty-headed leisure of people sunbathing in the void of afternoon, our appearance is an event: all of them, as if driven by a single spring, bounce up from the sand and run towards us, shouting hello and waving their arms. Up we shoot and then down we drop, swivelling in every direction, darting here and there in space as the fancy takes us, tracing with our motion through the air an incomprehensible hieroglyphic. And finally, we head back towards the city, along roads already crowded with cars returning to town on Sunday afternoon, a swelling procession of vehicles, towards the welter of houses and the labyrinth of terraces. Once again, we have the city beneath us, like the endless series of words in a speech; and the cheerful waves from windows, and people occupied in their countless acts and thoughts.

> One after laws and one to aphorisms
> Was going, and one following the priesthood,
> And one to reign by force or sophistry,
>
> And one in theft, and one in state affairs,
> One in the pleasures of the flesh involved
> Wearied himself, one gave himself to ease.[4]

And we were above there in the heavens.[5]

But it was late by now; already the outermost houses of the newly built quarters on the Via Salaria stood, like a grim wall drawing grimly back from the hovels of the shanty towns and the countryside; and the landing field was beneath us once again. Light as a cloud, we dropped down gradually, as if in a dream, questing here and there for the exact spot on which to land; there, earthbound again.

The skilled mechanics cluster around the helicopter, exchanging opinions and greetings, and we are back, back in the weight, the gravity, the surface, the tiresome space of the adult age.

CHAPTER VI

Apparitions in Rome

Things appear, draw near, show themselves to the eye, linger for a while, and then slip away in a blink of the eye or a turn of the head, in various ways, in distinct styles, at specific rhythms in different places and lands. Rome is a city of apparitions: actual, living, substantial, specific, colourful apparitions: real things that become apparitions, you might say, precisely because of their remarkable realness, their abundant quality of existence. It is a city of apparitions, not dreams and phantoms, like the swarming Paris described by Baudelaire:

> City full of dreams,
> where phantoms in broad daylight cross paths with the stroller[1]

in the hazy air, grey and light blue, in the fog, in the pale enchantment of twilight. Here, however, in our sharp, clear air, apparitions have the physical immediacy of gods. In this air of an eternal Epiphany (and it is no accident that the *Befana*, or Epiphany, of the Piazza Navona is the biggest folk celebration of the year), Christmas regains its age-old atmosphere, its luminous sky, its guiding star, the wintry warmth of the desert, the waterless horizon, its impoverished simplicity, from the time before it became a festival of woods and forests, full of black pines and firs, glistening white snow and cosy interiors. The thousands of trees on sale everywhere and the artificial snow with which they are sprinkled are not enough to conceal the older image of nomadic and pastoral sands, tents, and refuge taken in whatever manger presents itself, by those who are homeless in the great emptiness. In the crowded streets, brightly lit and elegantly adorned, ancient shepherd kings stroll by, with great nonchalance, playing their pipes. And, in sudden, entirely unforeseen ways, the gifts of the East begin to arrive.

It is late at night: one of those clear nights when the street lights echo a certain muted luminosity of the sky and the profound blue-black of the darkness is phosphorescent, like the still sea of a September evening. Strollers walk through the empty streets as if they were crossing a stage. Suddenly, an enormous lorry emerges from the shadows and slowly inches its way down the Via Capo le Case. The lorry is covered, practically enveloped by its cargo, which bulges out at the sides, concealing them, and looms high into the air, above the first few storeys: a load of thousands and thousands of balloons, all identical, all the same magenta red in colour as the ink of ballpoint pens, transparent, swaying, airy, translucent, light and, at the same time, immense. The lorry inches slowly downhill, as if moving gingerly with a priceless cargo, swaying as if pushed by the wind. It turns into the street that leads down to the Piazza di Spagna, seemingly filling the width of the street, moving ponderously around the Barcaccia, and then rumbles off, its red cargo brimming over and fading softly into the shadows, finally, almost indistinguishable, just tingeing the darkness.

This remarkable apparition, in itself, evokes and links to a thousand other images. It is an enormous cluster of grapes; grapes fit for giants, each morsel of fruit swollen with nectar from the Promised Land. It is a flag fluttering in the breeze, a forest of a thousand banners, an entire flag-draped people parading along the streets. It is a flickering, dancing flame, moving on its own, without burning, over the paving. It is the colour of distant, exotic, mysterious lands, the colour of India and China, swarming with people, carried here over boundless deserts. It is the light of chilly red stars over a broad, snow-covered square. It is the azalea festival on the steps of Trinità dei Monti, a red river that descends in silent cascades between its stone banks. And at the same time, it is the red balloons twisting and turning in the shooting galleries of the Piazza Navona, behind the girls who hand you a rifle. (One of the girls once, when she saw that I was a pretty good marksman, asked me to shoot at a balloon that she held in her hand.) It is a grape harvest, along the roads running between the rows of vines, with vans loaded with grapes, the aroma of grape must, and distant singing. It is a baroque sculpture, swollen, sensual, tender, curving, spectacular: a baroque sculpture made of air, carried in procession, like a sacred image, between the baroque stone architecture. It appeared, with all its implications, and by now it is nothing more than a vague and persistent image, a red mingling in the darkness.

Rome is a city of apparitions: actual, living, substantial, specific, colourful apparitions

And as you drive through the night, here and there in Rome, you find parts of that enormous cargo of balloons everywhere. Clusters of balloons have been tied all over the city, rising red against the night sky, from the top of street lights, from the uplifted arms of statues, from tree branches, from fountains, from cornices, from stone animals, from elephants, and from heraldic she-wolves that turn, craning their necks, fierce and maternal. The red of those balloons is the same red that appears to us through our closed eyelids, when we lie, heads on pillows, abandoning ourselves to sleep.

The next morning, when we awaken, there is another apparition. The world seems suddenly altered, along with the air and the atmosphere and our feelings, and their image. Rain drops silently over the trees in the garden, tender in the grey light. This is not the rain to which we are accustomed, pummelling, resounding, impetuous. This is a rain of great timidity and kindly restraint, dropping on to the leaves without moving them, as if fearful of committing some indiscretion, gentle, fond, modest; and it lovingly bathes the earth, almost without touching it. Not a branch sways, not a bird rises into the still air; a light, fresh youthful scent spreads through the park. In the reawakening dawn, this rain of childhood, with its gentle aloofness, proud and adolescent, takes me elsewhere, to other places, other times, to a distant springtime Turin, the eighteenth-century dew of a morning in the life of a young Goethe, before there was such a country as Italy.

Already, however, in the same silence in which it arrived, the rain flees before clear rays of sunlight, a fleeting apparition of other lands that have other rains, other suns, other histories, other sentiments. The grey melts into light blue, pure and clear again. Shadows add volume to the light and, through the newly crystalline air, monotonous laments come, dry and adult, from a distance, like flocks of sheep bleating on the arid slopes of deserted mountains, in the solitary pastoral vastness: the whining Christmas laments of the pipers.

CHAPTER VII

The Duty of the Comet

The comet, with its hazy head, like a tear-dimmed eye, and its tail tossing behind it in the winds of space, is hurtling, they say, through the heavens at an immense speed, climbing from the horizon up through the constellations until it vanishes somewhere in the firmament. I have not seen it myself. Springtime in Rome is so delicately wreathed in mist, fickle banks of cloud, sudden showers of rain, making the earth's atmosphere so intense and alive and youthful, so overwhelming the little movement here, that what takes place higher up eludes our gaze. I haven't seen the comet, nor have the Romans.

And they haven't made much of a point of trying to see it. You might say, perhaps, that they no longer believe in heaven, in signs from the sky, in the flight of birds, or in omens, as they once did. They don't even look up for rainbows that arch so wonderfully over church domes, standing out brilliantly against the soft violet of the plaster walls and the pale warmth of the travertine. Sometimes rainbows are mysteriously solemn in appearance, such as the double rainbow that I saw appear above St Peter's Square, like an unexpected sign or a divine ornament, high above the heads of an immense crowd with downcast eyes. Seated on terraces, the only thing Romans watch with patient pleasure are the long, drawn-out sunsets: that red, that purple, sacred vestments draping the horizon, are a wonderful spectacle, attracting the eye with their loveliness and with the lazy ease of their transformation into the blue velvet of night.

So we have not yet seen the new comet and it has not been the subject of much conversation. Nor is its arrival feared as a bellwether of impending disasters, as was the case so many years ago, when Halley's Comet held sway over the summer sky and over the consciences of one and all, immense and dusky red, with a great tousled menacing tail. That is how I remember it, wandering across the highest reaches of the sky of my childhood (whether an authentic memory, or a later reimagining), in that final dwindling of the years of peace, just before the world – beneath the comet's bloody gaze – itself roiled and split, hurtling, like the comet, who knows where. Perhaps people's consciences are more confident nowadays, because, unhappy as they are, they no longer fear the jealousy of the gods: or else science has rendered all these astounding phenomena familiar to the masses and science fiction has populated the constellations, in the minds of the young, with Disneyesque characters. Or perhaps too many aeroplanes freighted down with real death and real power have streaked across the sky, and now those imaginary influences seem too weak and too distant. And so the comet has been stripped of its powers. All that remains is its solitude, its irregular course: a lonely, mysterious traveller, isolated from every fixed system, wandering outside the web of rules and customs. Perhaps for this reason, in times of peace and stability, its image was linked to the image of war, the greatest possible interruption of the usual order of things. It seemed to trigger the age-old warmongering instinct, slumbering beneath the fear and revulsion at its horrors, but still latent in remote depths, like some irrational thirst for an escape from civil, ordinary existence. But, now that the idea and the image of war seem to accompany, like a shadow, the objects and even the actions of daily life, weighing down the appearance of things with their fog, perhaps the comet could (even though we remain content not to have seen it) change and reverse its symbolic meaning, turning its powers to the pursuit of good, so that we would welcome it heartily. Or, maybe, it will be looked at merely as an innocent, celestial, fraternal image of the desire for escape and change, the quest for elsewhere, which everywhere drives men on to roads, trains, aeroplanes, journeys, into an immense, incessant, whirlpool of movement.

Cities are empty during holidays and weekends. The more actively modern they are, the emptier they become. An old-fashioned Roman, a member of the ancient plebeians, would never leave his timeworn streets, except perhaps to venture outside the city walls, if fine weather beckoned, to a country inn. But a technician, a factory worker, a white-collar worker in the industrial cities of the north can hardly wait for the factories and offices to shut down, before he climbs into the hippogriff of his vehicle and sets off, to the delightful sound of its mechanical whinnying, in pursuit of the fantasy of elsewhere. The tarmac roads that lead to the mountains or the beaches swarm with motor scooters and small cars: the city is empty and, in the bright sunlight, seems haunted; the empty trams run screeching along their tracks, down streets that are too broad, as if they were running themselves. The exodus into nature is no longer merely a pastime, a sport, a whim, now it is something more: it is perceived as a duty. One might say that the weekly world of work is bound up with the ancient biblical image of sin; that the sweat of our brows entails the presence of the original Fall. That simple country leisure therefore implies, in some sense, the value of a return, or a redemption, to a time before evil, to an innocent earthly paradise. It is no longer the eighteenth-century myth of nature and the 'noble savage': rather it is an affirmation of self and a kind of collective rite

… the comet has been stripped of its powers. All that remains is its solitude, its irregular course: a lonely, mysterious traveller, isolated from every fixed system, wandering outside the web of rules and customs

of purification, from which no one is exempt. Those who stay in the city during holidays and weekends feel guilty, as if they had not only lost the pleasure of the life-giving air of the mountains or the forest, the loveliness of open fields and bright sunshine, but also as if they had evaded (or had been unable to fulfil) a dictate of their conscience. These Sunday journeys are, of course, short, as required by time and resources; even though we may happen to find in them, alas, nothing more than our own self and our own ennui, they are still immense journeys, journeys to another world. To an imaginary world of freedom without sin; to a collective world of individual freedom. Everyone gets up and goes, and everyone goes to the same places: but motor vehicles, this modern form of medieval isolation, available to one and all, offer everyone the same privileged solitude. Our feet never touch the ground and, faster than human beings, we can rush towards nature, in the midst of the crowd of other hurtling celestial bodies, along the milky ways, like so many little comets with smoky trails behind us.

The true travellers, of course, are another matter.

> But the true travellers are only those who depart for departure's sake.[1]

And yet even they, who set out in their thousands, as if to fulfil a duty, are driven, like the others, in their tiny adventures, by a sense of solitary risk. Seeing things (even the most ordinary and undistinguished things) by oneself is enough, with a shift of perspective, to make them new and true; to engender, by a change in point of view, an unconditioned reality. (Thus, in old treatises on painting, it is recommended to look at paintings with your head upside down and between your legs.) The setting or context of a journey is like that of a theatre. Things taken outside their usual context acquire an internal violence. It does not really matter whether the violence in question is a violent interest, a violent pleasure, or an equally violent boredom or disgust. It really doesn't matter where you go.

But holidays come to an end. For another week, angels with fiery swords stand guard at the city gates. 'But the feast day is followed/by the humdrum day'.[2] The thousands and thousands of temporary, intermittent comets return to the tedium of their daily orbits. But high above us, in the sky, the invisible comet leaves for good, fleeing forever into the freedom of the black abyss.

CHAPTER VIII

Elegy to the Mid-August Holidays

Tomorrow, to welcome August
I invite you, o lovely Elpina:
We shall drink a noble wine,
The fresh pride of my cellar.[1]

How times have changed! Where shall we ever find grapes bursting with such freshness, unless they are the golden transparent *luglienga* grapes that are so rare?[2] And vats, seething after grape-pressing ceremonies performed, in competition with villagers, by the townspeople who have taken up residence in the villa, their feet carefully washed and the turn-ups of their trousers carefully rolled up? And, indeed, where has the 'fad for holidays'* vanished, having survived the entire century after its heyday in the eighteenth century and the glory days celebrated by Goldoni, practically until the day before yesterday? The preparations, the debts, the jealousies, the envies, the discussions about servants, the games, the waters, the hangers-on, the false departures, and the decorum? This was a time when the custom of holidaying in the countryside was exclusive to the nobility and the wealthy, while the others, the petite bourgeoisie, simply tagged along, imitating, holidaymaking being the exclusive domain of a single class. Alongside them a faceless populace lived in the obscurity of the city without seasons. (Giorgio Strehler may have taken

* [*Translator's note*. A reference to the play *Le smanie per la villeggiatura* ('The Fad for Holidays') by Carlo Goldoni (1707–93). The play is part of the *villeggiatura* trilogy, which satirized the aristocratic fashion for taking summer holidays in the country.]

this as the inspiration for his version of Goldoni, in which the aristocratic class resembles the Gods of Valhalla, its deeds swelling into those of giants, on the eve of a revolution which appears, in the imagined background, as a Wagnerian twilight of the Gods.)

Now, perhaps, matters are reversed. The entire populace of the cities (it is a privilege, a great and genuine conquest), for at least a week, at least a day, migrates elsewhere, into the crowded teeming countryside. The empty city remains the only true countryside, the only unpopulated solitary land, and there alone is it possible to conceal oneself or, thoughtful and alone, walk the length, 'with slow, dragging steps', of the asphalt deserts, a Petrarchan strand unmarred by human footprints.[3] And just as on an ocean shore, when the tide gradually recedes, the motion of the waters, at first almost invisible, starts to gain speed with new rivulets and currents and pools in brief lapping waves, leaving more and more stretches of beach uncovered, in a shifting geography of islets, isthmuses, peninsulas, lakes, inlets, indentations, bodies of water in motion, until everything combines in a uniform expanse covered with seaweed and seashells, where crabs cheerfully scurry to and fro, on the last patches of moisture; and the sea, edged with waves and foam, is far off; likewise, day by day, with the exodus of the inhabitants, the city empties and changes, revealing a different self, until that day in the middle of August, when nothing passes over the desolate piazzas but the rays of the sun and the tumultuous, wave-swept world of people draws far away, leaving behind it the mineral and motionless enchantment of architecture, while the swallows fly giddily overhead.

City dwellers venture ever further, in ever greater numbers and groups, in a quest for nature. And nature, everywhere ravished, unveiled, and trodden upon, as if in a game of hide-and-seek, conceals herself in the ravines of the alleyways, peeks out from between palazzi, and spreads out in the empty heart of the cities. Already, in these few days prior, and preparatory, to the solitary recurrence of *Ferragosto*, or the feast of the Assumption, crickets chirp on baroque cornices, scorpions venture out from beneath terracotta roof tiles; and geckoes, those tiny endearing hybrids of crocodiles and tigers, pad silently on top of the walls, waiting in ambush for butterflies.

Rome, of all cities, is the quickest and best suited to this natural metamorphosis. Here, where it seems that nothing ever happens in the present, where everything seems to arrive as an echo reverberating through an age-old civic filter of history (an echo of events that occurred elsewhere, of the wars and revolutions fought by others, the muted echo of winds that blow elsewhere, of rains that fell on distant soils) a silence is enough to revive the deep past. A moment of solitude suffices to reveal a naked and solemn nature, always ready to seize ownership of the ruins. People too seem to fall under this ancient spell. Stretched out on the lawns of the parks, in poses as natural as if no eye could see them, they drift into a sun-baked animal state of sleep, undisturbed by the droning of aeroplanes, so many insects flying through the clear blue sky. And the architecture rediscovers itself, its inner baroque and plant-like self, its leaves, branches, and tangles; its rocky nature, violet, pink, and grey, stacked and dizzying, ready to greet the sun, modulating the sunshine with shadows, concealing the sunshine in cracks and fissures, reflecting it differently depending on the time of day; in the waves of baking heat, or in the courtly and comforting west wind; purpling and golden in the light of sunset; whitened by moonlight; vanishing into the blue velvet of night-time.

The empty city remains the only true countryside, the only unpopulated solitary land, and there alone is it possible to conceal oneself

Those who stay behind, in these days consecrated to the popular deities of crowding and collective holidaymaking, of busy leisure, tumultuous and companionable, can look upon this urban landscape as something intact, with the eyes of an ancient traveller who chances upon a new land, unseen by human eyes. Intent upon our discoveries, we wander curiously, in the lovely silence, among colonnades that have reverted to forest, the solitary cool of churches that have once again become grottoes, fountains with splashing water where real stone lions drink thirstily, unsuspecting.

Wild herbs grow on rooftops; flowers abandoned on terraces and balconies bemoan their parched neglect, and turn feral; birds wheel slowly overhead, fierce and gleeful masters of the sky. The city of men has gone elsewhere, to the beaches and the mountains, taking with it its customs, its tensions, its din. Here only space remains (shutters closed, telephones stilled), the arcane world of memory; the changeless shell of things; a seashell full of the rustling sound of the sea, on the uninhabited strand. Here, alone, we remain.[4]

CHAPTER IX

Hyperbolic Tourism

At this very moment, as I sit at my writing desk, pen in hand, carefully composing these lines, word by word, in the damp, heavy air of a late-summer sirocco in Rome, friends and acquaintances (except for those who have been tucked up in bed with the Asian flu) are travelling in far-flung lands. One friend is in Japan, another is in America, while others still are in China, or Persia, or Ghana, or in some other remote corner of the planet. Phones ring unanswered in empty rooms: trains, ships, and high-speed aeroplanes bear them all far from home, among foreign peoples, beneath unfamiliar skies: as each takes one of the thousands of opportunities offered in this time of travel and commerce; conferences, delegations, tour groups. And in exchange, monstrous tour buses invade, like glistening swarms of cockroaches, the age-old streets of Rome, vomiting forth on to the pavements from their metal wombs, like so many Trojan horses, the faceless warriors of mass tourism.

They crowd streets, piazzas, churches: they scurry everywhere, an infestation of ants. And no one can really say what drives them all, spontaneously, to leave their far-away homes and subject themselves to the discomfort and expense of a long journey, with no particular need or goal. Is it the inborn and perennial desire to see and learn? Or perhaps an abstract urge towards movement and change? Or perhaps a latent and emerging migratory instinct, left fallow and forgotten for years and centuries, like those found among certain animals which, when a certain season arrives, must suddenly stir and depart? Or, rather than any cognitive or rational or instinctive motives, could the fundamental reason underlying these organized, collective transmigrations be moral in nature, with its roots in mere conformism, a need to be like others, to do what others do, to have what others have; and to do, have, and be all together? Certainly, in that flock of travellers, it is difficult to imagine individual motivations (even though they may well exist); and it would appear reasonable to consider these crowds, in their numerical and external aspects, as a phenomenon of nature, a fit topic for the attention of scientists.

What do these collective assemblies of observers see, with their multiple eyes, all focusing, at the same angle, on the same things? Probably nothing, or almost nothing. Not that they go 'holding down their eyes and nostrils':[1] indeed their impudent gazes are redoubled, multiplied by cameras. A friend of mine, as a pastime, developed a diagram, or perhaps we should say, a law describing what can be seen by a traveller. He has named this law (and we shall see why) the 'first law of hyperbolic tourism'. The number of things, he posits, that a tourist is able to see is inversely proportional to the number of members making up the group. Someone travelling alone, therefore, will see, within the context of his own capacity for observation, his culture, and his personal interests, everything upon which he focuses his attention. If there are two travellers, each one will be able to see no more than half of these things; a quarter of them if there are four travellers; a tenth if there are ten; a hundredth if there are one hundred; and so on ad infinitum. If we plot on one axis the number of objects and on the other axis the number of observers, the curve that allows us to represent this law will be a branch of equilateral hyperbola with asymptotic axes.

The mathematical values of this curve will always be positive. But the psychological values that they express in numbers will quickly become negative, as the number of observers grows: since nothing more than a fraction of reality, increasingly fragmented and microscopic, will be perceptible, its value will in fact decline below zero with respect to reality as a whole. Hence the intolerable unease of group tours.

This equilateral hyperbola thus defines, in absolute terms, what can be seen and understood as a function of the number of eyes looking at the same things (including in their number the eye of the camera; and excluding from the calculation, of course, or including them only as fractions, the travelling companions who do not look at things, such as servants, or those who may happen to have entirely different interests). According to this law, the only journeys that allow us to learn and understand anything at all are journeys undertaken alone, far better than travelling in company, however limited and select. Goethe, or President de Brosses, or Stendhal, or any of those who have made their travels a tool of discovery and understanding, for themselves or for others, have always travelled alone.

Monstrous tour buses invade, like glistening swarms of cockroaches, the age-old streets of Rome, vomiting forth on to the pavements ... the faceless warriors of mass tourism.

If, rather than its value in terms of understanding, we choose to consider the pleasure derived from travel, countless other elements will be brought to bear. Countless other unknowns will modify that hyperbolic curve: modifying it in one direction or another in accordance with the varying quality of the travelling companions and their relationships. For most of the travellers who throng the streets, it would seem that their sole pleasure is that of companionship. This law can be applied to them, who see nothing, but it is of no interest (and can even be considered as a corollary to the general principle whereby every group aligns with its lowest component element). The very first voyage of discovery, which we all experience, as we journey from non-existence to existence – birth – is, by its very nature, a solitary journey.

If, instead of people, we turn our attention to things, we might say that they take on greater substance and value, the greater the number of eyes that, over the course of time (over the course of time, not at once), are laid upon them and have gazed at them. It is as if these gazes progressively enriched them, completed them, constructed them, and filled them with meaning and history. A virgin, barbarous, savage landscape has something intrinsically non-existent about it, something elusive and unreal: it lacks a name, it lacks certainty: because the eyes that look at things are always, for those things, the eyes of the divine. The works of man, made as they are to be looked upon, tend to grow over time. And some of those works, chosen to be loved, glow with more light than others, as if reflecting in all directions the countless gazes that have been fixed upon them: they are more real than others, more visible, more evident. They are so evident that they alone appear in the narrow field of vision of group travellers, and they will remain, for them, the names, the empty symbols, the idols of their blind journey: and their true value, having been established through the power of discovery, will continue to exist in the shape of conformism. Those with imagination, then, are better served (and laziness is not at issue here) by maps; and, like Ariosto, they may recline at their ease, travelling 'with Ptolemy, whether the world is at peace or war'.[2]

Alone, we depart. The aeroplane rushes across the airfield: we are aloft, elsewhere, free of all ties, our eyes watchful, ready to see the unknown.

CHAPTER X

Killing Time

In this eternal city of Rome, the people, as if by an ancient inclination, are accustomed to watching time go by, without false expectations, as if it were a long-familiar spectacle, a puppet show, observed as if in a theatre. Here everything, even the festivals – New Year, Epiphany, the feast of St John – and the football matches between the Roma and the Lazio teams, seems to happen as if in a duel, a street brawl, with wholesale destruction and countless insults. There are certain things, more than anything else, that Romans attack and insult: time, because everyone knows that time is eternal and indifferent; death, because of its silence and because the dead no longer play a role in the theatre of the world, the dead have the misfortune of not existing, the dead are empty, deserted; football referees (and isn't time, after all, the referee of all things?); broken things, because they are dead. 'We'll have to rip out everything,' say plumbers and electricians, no matter what they may have been summoned to repair, with expressions of joyous ferocity.

More than any other festival, New Year is a battle. For those who are normally busy wasting time, this is the thrilling moment in which they can kill time for real, with ear-splitting violence. The old year, finished and dead, is flushed out, chased down, insulted, persecuted, tortured, murdered: old objects are shattered with barbarous delight. From the high terrace upon which I hear the clock strike midnight, I see all of Rome spread out before me in the honeyed air: a sky that seems filled with fleecy lambs, with a sliver of moon arching over the black and purpling expanse of terraces and domes, fireworks, shouts, sirens, whistles, screams, general noise, shots, bangers – with names such as *castagnole, tric-trac, mortaretti, botti* – and Catherine wheels, explosions near and far, a great battle breaking out in every direction, on every street, throughout the immense nocturnal expanse. People crowd every window, hands clutching explosives, shouting in excitement, with the faces of warriors in some great people's army. Everywhere, fires flare and smoulder, as if in some immense air raid: shattered crockery and broken glass litter the street paving, bonfires crackle and smoke against the walls of buildings.

This battle of noise and flame has been getting fiercer year by year. The police may issue prohibitions, but Rome answers back, louder and louder. The first time I saw it was right after the war, on the New Year's Eve that ushered in 1946. Arriving from Naples on one of the unreliable trains of the period, I left the station and was heading for a restaurant in the Via della Croce: midnight caught me right in the middle of the Piazza di Spagna. Objects were showering down from everywhere, guns were being fired from windows: Rome was still full of the weapons of wartime. The piazza was empty. Alone, in the middle of the square, a lone prostitute ran to and fro, caught in a dithering frenzy, like a panicky hen. I took her by the arm and pushed her, all of a tremble, against a wall, until the fiery bombardment began to subside. That was how I began that first year of peace.

But do we need to believe in this hunt for the year, in the black forest of time and the streets of Rome, amidst pieces of architecture that are the very symbols of time, amidst the nooks and crannies, the gorges, ravines, and statues? (Where is time hidden? Under the cornices, between the travertine columns, in the curves of the baroque scrollwork, under the domes? Or in the alleyways, in the leaky gutters, under the bridges? Somewhere in the Roman ruins, or inside church bells?) This ferocious, resounding, baying, explosive, thundering, howling, ear-splitting hunt, how real can it be? Time passes anyway. It's nothing but a vendetta, a game for grown-ups; in a sense, a ritual that no one really believes in.

The following morning, the city was caught up in the lethargy that comes on the heels of a heroic effort. I called a friend: a crossed line brought me into the midst of a conversation between two strangers. The raucous, distinctly Roman voices of two men: 'So, are you going to Mass? Shall we go together?' 'You're going? The years go by, and you're afraid of the Devil, aren't you, admit it, you're afraid! And at your age, anyone would be.' 'Well, let me put my coat on and I'll come down. Where are we going, the Gesù?' 'Let's go to Santa Maria what's-her-name, okay?' 'I'll see you downstairs.' As I was listening to this exchange, still lying comfortably in bed, Amelia, my housekeeper, came in. She usually comes to do housework and run errands from noon to four o'clock. Her towering, imperturbable peasant body seemed oddly nervous and flighty today. She was tired: she had woken at five to prepare the New Year's Day meal at her house ('a ten-egg puff pastry'): the day before, she had not ventured to ask me for the day off. She was hoping that I would wake up early and eat early, so that she could leave immediately, to get home in time. But I had slept in, upsetting her carefully laid plans. I asked her how she had welcomed in the New Year. 'At my sister's, in Trastevere, near my house. They were letting off bangers. They say they're killing the old year: what's that supposed to mean? What good does it do? Last year, I stayed in bed: I slept through it all. You know Mrs Felici, my neighbour? She was off her head: "Throw out

The old year, finished and dead, is flushed out, chased down, insulted, persecuted, tortured, murdered: old objects are shattered with barbarous delight.

the old year, kill it, kill it!" Sure, she was up to her neck in debt, and it was eating her up: "Throw it out, kill, kill!" On 11 February, she died. She had paid her debts. Me, I slept in; okay, I had the Asian flu and a bad case of it, but I'm still here. Sure! Kill this; kill that: when you die, you die; when you're born, you're born. I don't believe any of it; I don't even believe in the Acqua Paola any more.'

Amelia, usually so calm, was so worked up that I insisted she hurry home for her dinner, and I ignored all her stubborn, angry refusals ('It's too late! I don't care any more!'). I got out my car and drove her home. The old walls of Trastevere looked like dried flowers in the buttery air. The streets were still littered with shattered crockery, forgotten relics of the violence. A black-feathered bird perched on top of the white marble column dedicated to the poet Belli. Last night's mutiny (Rome's only revolution, a revolt against the city's true ruler, time itself) had ended (in victory, or defeat? It makes no difference). Time had been murdered, but it was back now, the same as before: as in every revolution, the new government is just as despotic and unjust as the old one. After the fury and the fray, hearts were at rest. Peace had returned, with Masses and meals and the tepid loveliness of January sunlight.

CHAPTER XI

Points of View

It is customary to say, among those who are considering a problem or debating a complex and controversial question, without any real intention of solving the matter, that 'it is all a matter of point of view'. This may be, at the same time, a declaration of tolerance, or an admission of indifference. Certainly, things are always complex, twofold, or many-layered; it is certainly quite a different matter, to use a culinary metaphor, to be the 'person doing the stuffing' or the 'food being stuffed' (that is to say, subject or object, master or servant, and so on). What one person considers the greatest good may be the worst of evils to another person: what is a mote in one person's eye may appear to another to be a beam, what one person may see as a glass half full is a glass half empty to another. But leaving aside these all too obvious reflections, it is not just a matter of the human condition; things can be objectively different and may possess a differing intensity and value merely because of a different situation, constitution, or way of doing things, or a different visual angle: literally, a different point of view.

Yesterday, to pay a call on a friend of mine, in a flat I had never visited before, I climbed an ancient staircase, imbued with that serious and solemn lack of pretension typical of the common folk of Rome, a modesty that possesses a certain beauty, age-old and yet quite alive. Once I reached the flat, high on the fifth floor, and looked out at the view from the terrace, my eyes took in, all at once, the most astonishing apparition that, I believe, can be seen in this city of Rome, itself one constant round of surprising apparitions.

However accustomed I may have become – through long years of experience, journeys to far-flung lands, a steady familiarity with art, and a general curiosity to discover new things – to seeing every sort of unexpected sight, what lay before my eyes was so perfect and so stunning that, like a sudden gust of wind, it filled me with an authentic sense of excitement; like all feelings of the sort, it possessed, at once, a physical quality and something that eluded words entirely.

My eyes took in, all at once, the most astonishing apparition that, I believe, can be seen in this city of Rome, itself one constant round of surprising apparitions.

I stood, looking out, high above the Piazza Navona: that lofty terrace lined up precisely with the centre of one of the long sides of the elliptical seashell, on a line with the fountain, the obelisk, and the portal in the facade of the church of Sant'Agnese. I think everyone is familiar with this piazza. It is one of the most celebrated spots on earth: one need only utter the name to evoke a picture in someone's mind, a picture that, for that very reason, tends to be common or conventional. But here, the picture was entirely new: the shape and hue of every single thing was different, different from what I had seen the thousand times I had passed through here before. The fountain that, from the ground, seems to break up into a hundred facets to those who stroll, slowly, around it or who bring a thirsty dog to drink from it, rose whole, solid, and sharp, in the circle of green water. The green had something youthful, and even exotic, about it; an imaginary Orient (the green – I managed to discern amongst my confusion, without finding words to frame the thought – that you will find in Persian miniatures, or the paintings of the Ajanta caves). The animals slaked their thirst in a natural manner in that forest green. The animals? Only memory, or my instinctive capacity of discernment, allowed me to see them, because, in reality, the fountain and the animals, the rocks, the figures, the palm trees, were all a compact whole, unbroken, white, and perfect, that culminated at every point in its outline in a harmonious gesture, in pure form, and in which all the details, stories, and descriptions were absorbed and contained. The paving of the piazza, with its pale-blue cobblestones, was like an immense *opus reticulatum* laid out upon the ground (the new Rome appearing as an ancient Rome, prostrate, trodden underfoot, and inhabitable). Moving freely upon this horizontal wall, as if in a colourful enchantment, were people, close, familiar, silent, and clearly picked out, as if in a dream. The piazza was an enclosed world, unmovable, fixed for all time: the line of the roofs concealed the infinite universe beyond. Everything was form, meaning, history made solid: high above it all, at the summit of the obelisk, perched the bronze dove with an olive branch in its beak, while other olive branches stood high on top of the bell towers of Sant'Agnese. In this olive grove seashell the sun made its home, enclosed and warm, in the heart of the stones.

The angle from which the eye lights upon things is an intrinsic component of our relationship with the world.

It was a magnificent sight: but why, I kept wondering, after gazing upon it at length, and never tiring of it, was the thrill of this sight so intense? It was all architecture, in much the same way that *The Divine Comedy* appears as architecture if you read it in one sitting (as I have done every time that I find myself locked in a prison cell), as a single story, in a single day. This too is a way of looking down (or reading) from high above, just as I looked down on the Piazza Navona from above. The angle from which the eye lights upon things is an intrinsic component of our relationship with the world. The eye gazing upwards is the eye of a son or daughter: it seeks a father, transcendence, or faith; an elongated Byzantine eye:

it is also the eye of saints, an eye that does not see, but only hopes. The eye that descends upon the world, or gazes at it horizontally, is the eye of fathers or brothers, the eye of understanding, or imagination, classical, penetrating, and open. We might say that with the accumulation of objective understanding in paintings the eye has gradually gazed further and further upwards, until it achieved the so-called 'inversion of planes' of modern painting (which, ultimately, in an act of self-contradiction, in a flight from self into abstraction, closed its eyes).

As for me, I am most comfortable with the visual angle that looks down upon things. Perhaps this is because, by pure chance, I have lived since I was born in elevated spots, or because in the moments in my life when I felt most alive I was always in mountain-top villages, or in houses perched high up, or perhaps it is a matter of natural constitution and character. The flat where I live now, which is on the ground floor, surrounded by trees, seems unreal and strange to me. Looking up from below at the lofty crowns of the pine trees I feel as if I were a root, or a hermit who lives on roots. Someone else might feel at their ease, protected, safe, guarded by those towering vegetal sentinels.

Those who are accustomed to turning their eyes upwards look downwards to consider themselves. Those who gaze down upon things raise their eyes from the spectacle of the world to see themselves and gaze up at the sky. Pride and humility manifest themselves in opposing ways, according to diverse faculties and diverse points of view.

The sky over the Piazza Navona was a light-blue dome over the architecture, the sun was dropping behind the rim of the houses, and the seashell of the piazza was filling with a palpable shadow and the vague sound of a distant sea.

CHAPTER XII

The Power of the Poor

From that mysterious world encamped around the city of Rome, like a grey army, under banners of rags, eternally awaiting admission and eternally held back by the stout walls of organized life, strange messengers venture forth continually, to the very doors of our houses. There are so many of them! The doorbell rings: a man appears, with some obscure matter stamped on his face, he speaks and tells his story. They are all driven by need, genuine basic need: even those who use their wiles and deception to live and who invent imaginary needs to satisfy their real ones.

Some of them wind up following us for years, as if in cahoots with pity and weakness. They establish with us a relationship whose human meaning they alone can determine, in their fleeting appearances at our front doors: because they hold the power in this relationship: the tawdry power of the poor.

M. is one of them. He appeared for the first time, in the venerable old Roman palazzo where I lived at the time, many years ago. Small, dusty, yellowish, with a tiny, almost bald head, sparsely lined with blondish hair, his moist, narrow eyes set in a gently sly face, and the bare and passive authority of complete poverty. He told me that he had just been released from prison, after spending time in a sanatorium (the two havens of the poor); that, prior to these involuntary stays, he had been a barber by profession; and he asked me for enough money to purchase the scissors, combs, and clippers he needed to resume his former trade. What did I care if this was the truth? He would come back, quite often, always with new requests and with a general air that became, each time, a little more resignedly familiar, as if by now we were joined by a shared fate, in which he agreed to take part and to which I, in some sense, also belonged and to his nothingness. 'How's it going?' he would ask me each time, in a friendly manner. 'Fine,' I would reply automatically until, one day, on a whim, or to break the routine, I happened to say to him instead, 'Badly.' 'Badly?' he asked, concerned and understanding. 'Badly? Things are going badly for you, too? Oh, poor sir, life is hard, isn't it? For you, too. It's tough. And are you broke, as well?' 'Almost,' I replied, drawn in by his compassionate tone, so heartfelt and sincere.

From that day on, he kept coming to see me as before, but now he began to treat me like a fellow victim of misfortune. 'Are things still going badly, my poor sir?' He would greet me with a sign of ineffable understanding, each time I opened the door to him. 'Very, very badly,' I would answer. His requests had now become slightly (very slightly) more modest, and were made in the discreet and confidential tone of voice of someone asking for almost impossible assistance from a fellow sufferer. And the fellow sufferer would feel, upon hearing his words, truly broke: and yet at the same time so liberated from boredom as to wish to be more generous towards this imagined fraternal creature.

During that same period, M. began to phone me, for the sole purpose of asking me, with sugary concern, if things were still going so badly and offering me his discreet condolences. Then I moved to another section of town and I believed that I had freed myself of him and all the other countless beggars who used to besiege me with requests up and down the steps of the old palazzo. But I had not even moved into my new house before M., with his saccharine pity, was knocking at my door and the phone was already ringing with his grey voice, dripping solidarity. (I had not had the experience of one elderly Neapolitan gentleman, the father-in-law, I believe, of Nitti, who each day, during his stroll, would meet a beggar, to whom he would give a few coins. When the old gentleman happened to move house, he explained to the beggar that he would be changing the route of his daily walk and, begging his pardon for the inconvenience, suggested that he come over to the other part of town where he would be walking. The beggar showed up on the first day and the second: but on the third day he told him, with a certain note of reproach: 'Your Excellency, you live too far away. Find yourself another beggar.')

Small, dusty, yellowish, with a tiny, almost bald head, sparsely lined with blondish hair, his moist, narrow eyes set in a gently sly face, and the bare and passive authority of complete poverty.

M. did not abandon me: but his visits continued to be, as they always had been, intermittent and separated by long, mysterious periods of absence. After one of these prolonged absences he appeared, with his usual honeyed, pitying smile, one hot afternoon last summer. He enquired, gently, about my unhappiness and then asked for 1,500 lire, for some need or other of his. I was working, I was in a hurry, it bothered me to be interrupted and I had no loose change. I showed him my wallet, which contained nothing but a 5,000-lire note. 'Is that all you have? Well, life is hard,' he said. 'I'll go and get some change, downstairs, from the doorman. I'll be right back. You hold on to my hat.' Before I could open my mouth, he was gone with my money, and he had left me in exchange a greasy slouch hat, which I hardly knew where to hang. Of course, he did not come back upstairs. M. was right: I should not have led him into temptation. I thought to myself that at very moderate cost I had freed myself forever of that strange accomplice who obliged me to don the garb of a mendicant.

But a few days ago, M. came back. Paler and greyer, and more tawdry, jaundiced, passive, and non-existent than before, to the point that I barely recognized him. In response to the obligatory scolding that I gave him for coming back to see me after his less-than-friendly deed, he answered, absently, that he had just been released from prison; and he left, with a few coins in hand, promising never to return. But the next day he phoned me: 'It's cold, and my head is bare. That hat of mine, did you throw it away, or did you keep it?' I had kept it, wrapped in paper. He came back to get it. He was still the compassionate fellow sufferer. After all, what does one deed or another matter, between us? We shared a destiny. 'I can't remember a thing,' he told me. 'My memory is gone. I have forgotten everything. You live here, in the middle of this garden. How nice! But I can't remember how it is that trees manage to grow. You should give me a book, so that I can go back and teach myself. Now I can't remember how plants are born.' He looked at me, with his moist, narrow eyes, with fondness, whether feigned or real. 'But you, my poor sir, you smoke too much. A few years ago, your teeth were so white! You looked like a black man. Blacks have teeth as white as snow.' And he was gone.

He will reappear, without a doubt, emerging for an instant from the shanty towns of non-existence, where he sleeps on the ground, in some corner, at the gates of the city: a shapeless witness to an invisible power.

CHAPTER XIII

Brigands and Peasants

One day, I will write the true story of my friend Antonio L., a peasant from Lucania and, as he calls himself, a 'folk author'. For that matter, he is already at work on the story himself, writing it out in a series of school exercise books that he keeps, with black oilcloth covers – just as many others do where he comes from, prompted by the example and inspiration of the autobiographies gathered by Rocco Scotellaro in his book *Contadini del Sud* ('Peasants of the South').[1] Couched in an unassuming prose style all of his own, his leisurely accounts describe the daily happenings of a remarkably differentiated society with its own internal code, like some obscure aristocracy, living in a village and on desolate soil, whose feelings, thoughts, reactions, and conceptions of the world could never be imagined, even in a work of pure imagination, by anyone who had not experienced and understood them, not even by the greatest of writers. In his village, Antonio is like a tree in a forest: surrounded by authentic relationships, age-old, solid bonds; every one of his acts forms part of a whole, and this whole is present, clear, and comprehensible. His folk songs are sung in the piazzas, or to the accompaniment of the accordion during convivial evenings in local homes, and these songs say things that are felt and thought by all who live in the shadow of this obscure dialect. Antonio's story, then, is a true story, one of the countless inner stories of the peasant world: his persona, in this world, is full of character, intelligence, and poetic value, and it is anything but simple.

But Antonio, like so many others, driven by unemployment, left his world and his village, secluded high on its hilltop, and came to Rome. He came in the hope of recording his songs, publishing his short stories, and, last of all, if possible, finding work of some kind to put bread on the table. Here another story begins, of an entirely different kind: a story of appearances and disguises. Here, Antonio (like everyone else in the world of the poor, in the eyes of the people of the capital) is no longer what he is, but rather what he appears to be: and he must act and react accordingly. The Romans look at him, consider him, study him, sniff warily at him, and condemn him. But he (sly as he is) knows how to defend himself, with a weapon that is ancient and judicious, at times even welcoming and brotherly, the weapon of distrust. Antonio knows everything and he knows how to conduct himself perfectly. But to others, in Rome, who is Antonio? A small man, round-headed, with wrinkled sunburnt skin, careful and reticent in his speech, with a courteous, astute smile, lively dark eyes, slow gestures, and the gait of another land where donkeys set the pace along the paths and trails, a heavy, threadbare suit, made of old and faded cloth, his shoes covered with mud and dust. He is a nobody, one of the poor. Over the course of just a few days, because of his appearance, the police had already stopped him on three separate occasions. They did their best (in vain) to trick him into stating that he had no money and no work, so that they could send him back to his village. But Antonio sidestepped their traps and knew how to avail himself of his rights as a citizen. Moreover, among those policemen, he is able to detect, with an infallible eye, that they are no different from him, Lucanian peasants, in a sense in disguise, and so they wind up speaking the same language: Antonio is still here.

After these three brushes with the law, Antonio had a fourth; this one was more dangerous. He came to see me yesterday and told me all about it. 'I was at the station,' he said to me (the railway station is the centre, the meeting place. It is also where you can try to get some sleep if you have nowhere to stay, it is a place to look for work; or just spend a few hours in a nameless, brotherly crowd, near the trains that arrive from down south). 'I was at the station: I go there every day. I was sitting down, I had nothing to do. Two policemen come up to me. "You, what's your name? What are you doing in Rome? Do you have identification?" "And who are you?" I reply. They show me their police identification. Then they start asking me, as usual, if I have work. I tell them that I am in town for business of my own, as a folk author. "Do you have means of support? Do you have money?" I tell them that I have lots of money: that I have a 10,000-lire note in my pocket. They start to chat with me and now their tone is friendly. They ask me if I am interested in finding work so that I can stay in Rome; they say that they can help me. "That would be both courteous and kind of you," I tell them. "Why not? Of course I'd like that." They talk amongst themselves for a little while. They were both Sicilian, one was skinny and slight, the other was built like a bull, with a leather bracelet on his wrist. They turn back to me: the little one tells me, "There might be a job, a good job, for you. We policemen know about these things. A job as a gardener for the nuns of Monte Mario. In a few minutes we'll be off duty; if you want, we could go out there right away; friends need to help one another. Would you like to go?" "Well, that's very kind of you: but why do you want to go to so much trouble?" So after all is said and done, we leave the station all together. They tell me we'll have to take a tram and then

These are the stories of life, appearances, and disguises, in the city of Rome, where poor brigands … walk around disguised as the law … trying fruitlessly to extort money, in the time-honoured tradition, from poor peasants, disguised as waiters.

a bus; we all get on together, they pay for the tickets, I never pay a lira, and, finally, after a long, long ride, we reach the top of Monte Mario. The big one says, "The convent is right there: I'll go in and talk to the Mother Superior: you stay here and wait, and, then, if everything works out, we'll introduce you and, with our recommendations, you will have yourself a nice little job." I stay with the little one. "An espresso?" he asks. He buys me a cup of coffee; I never pay for anything. After the coffee, he asks me if I'm hungry: it's about time to eat: he orders sausage, cheese, wine: a full meal. I hadn't eaten a thing since morning. The policeman, unfailingly kind, had ordered everything and paid for everything. After an hour, the big one comes back, with an old suitcase.

'"It's all taken care of. The Mother Superior agrees. All you have to do is show up the day after tomorrow and you have the job. All you have to do is ring the bell at that door over there, the door of the convent. You will like it here." I thank them for their generosity. "Now," says the little one, "there is only one thing left for you to do. You need to get your papers before the day after tomorrow. You need a certificate of residence." "Now what you are saying is wrong," I answer. "That doesn't sound right to me. I can't get a certificate of residence until I have a job." "Why worry about such a minor detail?" they say. "The Mother Superior is a strange character and she'll hire you right away, but she wants the certificate. Leave it to us. We are with the Forensic Unit, and we will arrange to get you the certificate. It's easy for us. Of course, there will be a charge for stamps, seals, legal documentation. It will cost you 10,000 lire." "Listen," I say to them, "you have been too kind and I will show you my gratitude once I have earned my first month's pay; and the same is true of the certificate: if you are willing to get me one, I will pay you for it once I have been paid." They talk a little amongst themselves, and then: "Well, we'll see. In the meantime, carry this suitcase for us: we need to go to Primavalle." We take another bus and then, on foot, we enter Primavalle: the suitcase is really heavy. Night falls. We keep walking until we come to a deserted little lane, and there they start asking me for the money for the certificate again. "Listen," I say. "Now that we are friends, I will tell you the truth. I don't have any money. The 10,000 lire I told you about, I never had that. I will pay you afterwards." They both look angry. "Truth for truth," says the little one, "you don't have any money and we aren't really policemen. We are a couple of robbers."

'We walk on a little further in that solitary lane. Now I'm really scared! I look around: no one in sight. The little one stares at me fiercely: "You've made us waste an entire day, and we've spent 2,000 lire on bus fares, coffee, and lunch! You owe us that much. If you have no money, then give us your overcoat. If you won't do as we say, then you'll never get home alive." And he starts to reach for me. I throw the suitcase to the ground: all stolen goods, of course. Luckily, the big one was a few steps behind us: he had sore feet because his shoes were too tight: stolen shoes. I give the little one a quick shove, and then run for it. I find a cafe and I hurry in, without looking back. My face was so pale that the owner asked me what was wrong; I told him that I didn't feel well: he made me a cup of coffee and didn't even ask for money. I stayed there for an hour, to make sure that the two robbers had left; then I took a bus and went back to the station.'

Thus ended Antonio's fourth encounter with the authorities, real or not. The next day, Antonio somehow found a job as a waiter. These are the stories of life, appearances, and disguises, in the city of Rome, where poor brigands, fallen on hard times, walk around disguised as the law, wearing painfully tight stolen shoes, trying fruitlessly to extort money, in the time-honoured tradition, from poor peasants, disguised as waiters. Where are the barren expanses of mountains, the boulders, the forests, the flocks, and the grim sky? Brigands and peasants await one another, at the station.

CHAPTER XIV

Plants and Seeds

There are things that stay in their places, occupy their particular spaces, and live their lives, so naturally and so truthfully that they are invisible. The everyday eye passes over them without quite seeing them. We walk past them, we look at them, and we fail to perceive them, perhaps because they are so much a part of the world, not distinct from the whole: like a column or a cornice, necessary and hidden, in a harmonious piece of architecture, or a single word that blends in with the rest of a complete sentence. To see them is a discovery, a leap into a different dimension of existence: when we do, another world opens up to us: the entirely real world of continuity.

I have lingered thousands of times in the Piazza Navona: but only yesterday, for the first time, as I stood in front of the fountain, did I see the small door of a tiny shop, only yesterday did I read a sign that said 'Plants and Seeds'. Little rose bushes, in terracotta planters, were arrayed on the steps in front of the door; cages with birds hung on either side of the entrance. It had been the whistling of a bird that made me raise my eyes to reveal that ancient door. They were canaries, yellow, pale, and grey: I entered with an idea of buying a few. Inside, in the dark recess, the smell of hemp sacks mingled with the earthy aroma, sun-baked and dry, of seeds. Huge sacks of white beans, or violet beans, or multicoloured beans, sacks of dried broad beans, of wheat, oats, chickpeas, green peas, *lupini* beans, grass peas, and millet, filled the shop. From behind the sacks the owner appeared: a sturdy old man, with a broad face and a large, meaty nose. He wore a dark suit, made of heavy cloth, and had a woollen scarf wrapped around his neck and a black hat on his head. He told me, wheezing as he spoke, that those birds were not for sale: they were his own birds, and he kept them because he liked them. His accent, his asthma, and his direct, humane, not to say philosophical, way of speaking, all revealed him to be a Neapolitan. 'They are canaries that sing beautifully,' he said, as he showed them to me. 'I breed them myself: you see the little newborns? Their song cheers me up: when I hear them, I feel as if I am in the country, not here. This one over here, this is the best singer of the lot: he is a hybrid of canary and goldfinch: he sings beautifully, but cannot reproduce. This other bird,' and he pointed to it, sitting alone in its cage, bigger than the others, dark-feathered, with a bold eye, 'is a tawny pipit. It can imitate every kind of birdsong, any sound at all. One day, I heard it respond to the song of a quail that had perched on that window across the way. To hear it, I thought that I had a quail right here, in my shop.' The words can't express what his face, his gestures, his wheezing conveyed. He was a king, contented with a humble domain all of his own, a realm of contemplation, complete, secure, poetic, and permanent in the great outside world. Friendly and supportive, he advised me, if I was interested in buying canaries, not to go to breeders or to pet shops, which were too expensive, but to go to a mechanic and cyclist, in the Via delle Colonnelle, who would sell me some lovely songbirds at a reasonable price, because he too was an enthusiast.

On my way out, I stopped to look again at the cages and the roses. The old man had disappeared amidst his sacks, in the back of the shop; at my side there appeared an old woman, petite, tiny, with sweet-natured dark eyes in her ancient face. 'If you want that rose bush, I will sell it to you for 700 lire. But don't let my husband hear, he would ask for more. We have everything we need: at night, when I go to bed, I want to fall asleep with a clear conscience. And may St Agatha protect me.' How kind she was, the aged Catanian wife of the Neapolitan shopkeeper! She too was an unassuming queen, with an earring at each ear, grey hair, the mistress of a tiny, unshakeable world, unchanging over time, an indissoluble and eternal fragment of the humble Italy, which asks for nothing, and just goes on living, in its peacefulness.

Across the way, beyond the alley, beneath the Arco della Pace, some children warm themselves by a fire burning on the ground. Written on the side of the exedra of the magnificent church of Santa Maria della Pace are the words 'orietur in diebus nostris/justitia et abundantia/ pacis/donec auferatur luna'.[1] That complete and unchanging world extends in a thousand different aspects in the little side streets, in the dark staircases, in the cloisters, in the workshops where age-old trades are practised, in the Roman intonations in the women's voices, in the games that children play on the flagstones of the Vicolo degli Osti or the Piazza di Montevecchio, in the white banners of tattered cloth strung between windows, in the rustic trophies of salamis and cheeses, piled in baroque mountains in the shop windows, in that populous maze where everything has peace in its name. Santa Maria della Pace is deep in shadow and silence. In the middle of the church, amidst statues and sepulchres, a young woman is kneeling, blonde and very beautiful. A black lace veil frames her face, setting off the faint blush of pink: her cloak drapes into exquisitely elegant folds: it is divine grace herself, come down into this humble world. But her dark eyes are moist from weeping: down her cheek a tear makes its mysterious way.

He was a king, contented with a humble domain all of his own, a realm of contemplation, complete, secure, poetic, and permanent in the great outside world.

Names count, names carry weight. Here peace covers a perfect, humble world with all its enchantment. On the far side of Rome (cars bear us at such dizzy speed over vast distances!) here I am, minutes later, paying a call on a friend, amidst new streets that all bear the name of some lost country of Africa: all that remains of a fledgling empire whose reach far exceeded its grasp. Via Fezzan, Via Amba Alagi, Via Scirè, Via Etiopia: huge new blocks of flats, paving stones without history, darkest barbarity. I stand in a piazza on which these African streets converge from every direction. The skyline, stark against an exotic background of grey clouds, is composed of buildings that seem like enormous tuculs, or Ethiopian circular houses, their roofs shaped like ambas, the flat-topped mountains of Ethiopia, painted in the muddy, violet hue of the skins of natives. Those names on the street corners form ill-omened desert landscapes. From the sky comes down a rain of mud: water tinged a Saharan creamy yellow.

Every street is crowded with shops, like so many colonial kiosks with neon lighting. The butchers display bloody meat, as if for cannibals, set amidst red tulips. The florists in these deserts call their shops 'Flowering Oasis'. Barbarous scents appear in the windows of beauty salons, along with 'Turtle Oil Anti-Wrinkle Cream'. In these inhospitable wastelands, the civilization that survives is sentimental. Establishments have names like 'House of La Mamma' and 'Children's Paradise'. Culture is to be found in the windows of the *cartolibrerie*, or the book-and-stationery shops. Since this is territory for missionaries, all the books are strictly edifying. Holy Scripture, *Lives of the Saints*, *Jesus's Mamma*, *I am the Way, the Truth, and the Life*, *The Day Christ Died*, and so on. There are other books, but all of them have at least an evangelical or missionary reference in their titles (and it hardly matters whether it is by chance or design): *Adventures in Paradise*, *The Band of Angels*, *A Detective Priest*, *Dark Angels*, *Christ among the Bricklayers*, *Forbidden Fruit*, *My Man Benito*; and books by Malaparte and Papini. The only other books are *The Story of a Poor Young Man*, *Little Women*, and *The Courtly Secretary*. This world, not yet finished, uncertain of whether it exists, thus finds its first cultural underpinnings. The streets, running between shops selling appliances, televisions, radios, various colonial boutiques, and the dusty cement desert, all converge on another piazza that takes the odd name of the monument that it houses. In the middle of the square, an anachronistic Roman ruin rises, like the temples of Cyrene surrounded by waterless sands. It is called the Sedia del Diavolo ('The Devil's Seat').

CHAPTER XV

The Steps of Rome

There are steps, in Rome, that are much more than a frontier, a wall, a boundary; that delineate and separate two distinct and different worlds, that stand as an ethical and material symbol, between the world outside and inside. These steps, for women, are the steps outside their front door. Behind the doorstep, in rooms brimming with warmth and clutter, where no eye can penetrate that is not part of the family (for the gaze of father, husband, or brother is not really a gaze at all; it is not a link with another, it does not stand out from the undifferentiated mass of the tribe, it is a commonplace of nature), women get ready to go out, to pass over that threshold, towards the street that belongs to others. Or they rest after coming in from outside, from the emotional exhaustion of having revealed themselves. Where the sun holds sway in the sky, fixing its cross on stones and architecture, it is natural that what happens is the opposite of the lands of the crescent moon. There, women are hidden from all eyes. They pass through the streets enclosed in impenetrable veils, drapes, cloaks, and armour, with invisible eyes peeping out from behind a loophole or a grate, inhuman shapeless things, cancelled from existence itself, entirely shut up, and devoted wholly to the secrets of home and harem. Here, it is in the home that women become objects, that they abandon their person, restrict their thoughts, willingly forget dreams and ambitions, gather their strength for the solemn moment in which they leave the house. They stand, wrapped in threadbare, faded dressing gowns, feet stuck in slippers, legs naked or draped in sagging stockings, their hair dishevelled or twisted beneath nets in the endless cocooning of clips and hair curlers and hair rollers, wrapped with cotton wool or newsprint, looking like stubble-covered fields after a Sunday afternoon picnic. Their voices are sharp with anger or dull with boredom, their gestures are tired and droopy, their feet shuffle as they walk, their expressions betray irritation or nausea. In this condition, restricted to the non-existent plane of the family, they would certainly not step out into the street, even just to go round the corner to buy a roll at the baker's. The caretaker's daughter, who is perhaps expecting a letter, peeps out from behind her front door to see if the postman has passed by yet. Once she reaches the sacred threshold, she stops, she steps hesitantly, like someone testing the water before plunging into the sea for a swim, then withdraws her foot hurriedly, cat-like, and scurries to take cover in her grotto, fearful that she has been spotted. A short while later, she re-emerges. But it is another person that emerges. The drooping shoulders are now erect and proud, her hair glitters with curls in the sunlight, her pale cheeks are now rosy pink, her lips are vividly red, like flowers, the eyes that were dulled with boredom now gleam with an angelic or diabolical light, her out-thrust bosom cleaves the air, her high heels tap on the pavement, making a music straight out of paradise, a body that is entirely lithe, youthful, vigorous, powerful, and glorious will parade through crowded streets, like a crystalline mirror in which every eye can admire itself. With the daily transmutation, the larva enclosed in its cocoon becomes a queenly butterfly and ventures out, regal and indifferent, into the realm of the outside world, into life. No Narcissus gazes at his reflection in the fountains, in the thousand fountains of Rome, so many baroque daughters of Narcissus. Love is beyond the steps: it is a grown-up love.

For men, at least for men who adhere to the ancient plebeian folk tradition, there are different steps, symbols of manliness and worth. 'In the prison of Regina Coeli there is a flight of steps/if you never climb it, you are no Roman.' There you enter, never to exit. But Rome, for men and for women, lies beyond those steps. Facades matter, they are the true walls of other people's lives (and of our own life), the walls of our real house. Intimacy lies without, just as life lies without. It is unlikely that the interior, the basis of modern architecture, could be understood here and become a reality. But the steps that divide the exterior from the interior are still a sign of love, a love that is so adult that it has entirely forgotten about childhood.

> A world are you, O Rome, but without love
> the world is not the world and neither can Rome be Rome.[1]

Faustina knew this (and taught this), as the young Goethe counted out the metre of his verses on her naked back. In that house on the Via del Corso, towards the Piazza del Popolo, in a section of the city that has remained practically untouched, perhaps protected by that love and by the love, invisible and more powerful, that belongs to poetry. Without love, Rome is no longer Rome: Indifference (with her handmaidens, Corruption, Speculation, and Bureaucracy) is tearing it down.

Throughout history, and perhaps to an even greater degree in the golden years of great architecture, destruction has been part of the process of beautifying and enlarging the city, creating a living city in the present for all time. Indeed, frequently, beautiful things were destroyed only to be replaced with things less beautiful, or even ugly or hideous. How many mediocre seventeenth-century facades have covered venerable Romanesque churches; how many pretentious palazzi have risen from the destruction of ancient ruins, still shrouded in a deathless enchantment! And yet, this was nothing more than an inevitable component of error that went hand in hand with splendid creations: the error that is proper to life, continually reabsorbed and levelled out in the general flow, in the larger continuity: in life, which also consists of forgetfulness, loss, destruction, and abandonment. And the fruit of this continuity, of this unbroken succession of good and evil, was a house built for one and all, with luminous walls, the magnificent seashell that is Rome, which withstands encrustations, Madreporaria, and parasites, without ever losing its harmonious form. Because, inevitably, a secure self-esteem, a love of one's own time, a confidence in a universal relationship, is the driving force, despite all chaos, in all growth, like one of those obscure and loving laws of vegetal symmetry, safeguarding the identity of the species, making that tree a tree and that flower a flower.

But the errors of the last few years have nothing to do with love and life. They are signs, depressing and anything but dialectical, of death. Every year, every day there pass through the streets, beyond the hearth, new flocks of young women and men, like migrating birds: an unceasing river of new generations who occupy, glorious tenants, this ancient land, bearing within them, in their slender and happy bodies, the physical miracle of continuity. But what surrounds them, bit by bit, is no longer their home, no longer the true walls of their earthly abode, lived-in and changeable. It resembles, in its drabness, holiday suites, their empty, mechanical, furnished, conventional world, a universe of cleaning, petty jealousies, scrimping, worries, and matters dark and unspeakable. The hidden, non-existent world that dominates high on its hill and makes decisions for everyone, fixated upon the advantages to its own position, creates and then disposes of its regulatory plans. That world triumphed once before with Fascism, and it left its indelible marks: streets paved with the word 'Duce', and the male nudes and obelisks of the Foro Mussolini. But the worst of these passionless crimes is the Piazza Augusto Imperatore, the Via del Mare, which goes all the way out to the Via della Conciliazione. Then came the smothering carpet of cement in the new quarters and the destruction of parks and villas: the sole endeavour, the sole ideal, was speculation. The deliberations of the city council over the past few months, the affairs of the parks, the Hilton hotel, and the regulatory plan could serve as fodder for a moralist author. What has emerged and continues to emerge is not only bad, ugly architecture, devoid of historic and poetic continuity. What we are witnessing are agencies, mysterious forces: relics of history, shameful history. The most obvious symbol of these deeds would seem to be the EUR (Esposizione Universale di Roma), this senseless collection of fake buildings (erected, as the inscription states, for 'a people of saints, navigators, and heroes'), for which no one can find the slightest real use, but which, transformed into some occult authority, exerts its influence on the life and development of Rome. The plan, from what I hear, is to put the national library there: and so, culture, banished to that land of the dead, may perhaps aspire to serve some purpose or someone, bringing its benefits to earth, that is, to its real estate value.

With the daily transmutation, the larva enclosed in its cocoon becomes a queenly butterfly and ventures out, regal and indifferent, into the realm of the outside world, into life.

Thus the house of one and all, with its facades and its streets, its alleys, and the unexpected apparitions of another time, the live budding forest, and nature and history, constantly present, tends to become an anthill, a cemetery. Until we decide once and for all to take that gentle flight of steps that is liberty, the meaning of the state, that flight of steps that unites, and without which 'the world is not the world and neither can Rome be Rome.'

CHAPTER XVI

The Empty Cities

The sun rides high above, in the middle of the sky, motionless and invisible like a king. It is the midday of midsummer, the middle of the year, the middle of the century, the middle, perhaps, of life. Everything is at a standstill, shadowless; everything is white and glistening. Is everything love, or is everything emptiness?

Beneath the sun that penetrates everywhere, right down into the grottoes and the crevices of the alleys, and seems to fill every available space, every cavity, lie the empty cities. Abandoned by their inhabitants, left alone to their nature of stones, shapes, air, dimensions, solidity, crystallized history, they seem new and different, practically unrecognizable. Why are they so strange and almost moving? So much so that they have been luring me, driving me, over the last few days, through blisteringly and blindingly hot streets and squares, as if to an extraordinary spectacle.

In a city as ancient as Rome, one might think that the enchantment of the emptiness during *Ferragosto*, or the feast of the Assumption, lies in a pleasure of the imagination which, freed from the presence of the modern-day crowd, the cars, the machinery, the noise, the life of today, seems to recapture the image of the true past of the architecture, rejoicing in this return. It is an understandable fantasy, but it is baseless and historically false. The days of the nineteenth century, the days of the other centuries that we love to evoke, were anything but empty. They were crowded with a different life, a life that made facades and elevations different as well; the days of ancient Rome were probably teeming with life, like a day spent nowadays in an Indian bazaar. An empty city does not reproduce an unrepeatable past, even if, by freeing us from the present, it can unchain our imagination.

Even the late-night cafes were closed for cleaning; the tired women had abandoned the pavements; and birds had begun to sing in the trees along the boulevards. Our steps echoed down the long streets, with the thrilling sound of solitude.

For that matter, we can procure this image of the empty city any day of the year, if we happen to step outside, or return home, at that dawn hour when everything is shut up and motionless in the grey light. Even the houses seem like so many sleeping birds, and anyone who, all alone, is awake and on the move is the new master of all space. I once chanced to discover a Paris I had never seen, by crossing the entire city on foot early one May morning, a still, architectural Paris, like a vast rational plan that life normally conceals, where everything that is hidden, implicit, and tacit by day, becomes suddenly explicit and evident. At that hour, the last trains of the metro and the last buses had gone by, and the first had not yet started their runs. Even the late-night cafes were closed for cleaning; the tired women had abandoned the pavements; and birds had begun to sing in the trees along the boulevards. Our steps echoed down the long streets, with the thrilling sound of solitude. Everything, even the old flaking buildings, the decrepit little hotels, the over-opulent facades, everything was lovely. Even the Madeleine seemed beautiful, like a Greek temple translated into a courtier's dialect. And Baron Haussmann[1] is a genius of the rational. But, before we reached the furthest house at the other end of the city, in the earliest rays of sunlight men began emerging from their homes, rubbing their eyes, their work tools in hand. Rome, at that delicate hour, which I see quite often, is tender and marvellous. The architecture has weight and splendour; the natural and subterranean world calmly takes over, establishing its blood ties to the stones of mythology, filling with apparitions and enchantments, in the silvery light of a green forest.

The emptiness of these hours is different from the emptiness of the days around *Ferragosto* in mid-August. You sense that everything is in a state of suspension, but is about to begin. The inhabitants have fled into sleep, hidden, as if dead: but already a yawn, a sigh, the sound of work hints at the new day: the abandonment is natural, involuntary, and has nothing of the ritual about it.

But at *Ferragosto* the abandonment is a rite: a festive rite, with certain funereal implications. Everyone flees the city, as if the plague had broken out, or as if the city housed some sacred object of fear: only a few of the laity are allowed to remain, or the poor, or godless tourists, who are foreigners and barbarians. Whether the origins of this great collective migration are religious in some recondite manner, or whether they just seem so precisely because it is a collective phenomenon, a shared action that springs from shared needs, its appearance and its nature are that of a ritual. It is a ritual that has something in common with the rituals of the seasons and the harvests, or with the funereal laments of the vegetal passion. (Ernesto De Martino describes this for us in his lovely book *Morte e pianto rituale nel mondo antico* ('Death and Mourning in the Ancient World'),[2] which I am reading right now and about which I will write at greater length another time.) One might think that the motif of alienation, the danger to the presence posed by the mechanical, monotonous work we do all year, by work as a penalty and a sin, somehow induced this ritual of flight and abandonment, which offers a collective form, and an established rhythm for rest, ritualizing the necessary renunciation to one's work, freeing one at once from labour and from guilt.

If we bear the guilt for the work of the sweat of our brow, we thus transfer it to the city. We punish the city, abandoning it light-heartedly and nonchalantly. We leave the city alone, inhabited only by a deity that dies during these days and will be reborn when we return. We leave the city deserted: no one collects the rubbish, which immediately begins to pile up on the pavements. (The run-aways celebrate their funereal orgies amidst the purifying baths of the seaside, or they perform worshipful ceremonies in high places.) In the guilty, dead city, abandoned to the vendetta of the sun, those who remain behind, along with the foreigners, idlers, the poor, and the poets, are the guardians of the sacred: caretakers, sitting in their chairs, in the cool of the alleyways, amidst the tumbling scraps of waste paper.

CHAPTER XVII

Girls and Trees

Springtime, in Rome, is adult at birth: you never see it, except in a few rare and fleeting instances, emerging chilled and vulnerable from the winter. When you do meet it, and you realize it, springtime is already fully grown, like certain boys who grow to be immense at an early age and who, though still playing like children, already tower over their parents. For some time now, the birds, in the trees of the park, have resumed singing. First one singing solo, then all the others joining in, at that moment of half-light just before dawn, when it seems as if the birds alone, in a slumbering world, beneath the last paling stars, are waiting, feathered prophets of an impending luminous birth. Then the sun glows upon the already confident greenery, pushing soft warm breezes through the blossom-scented air. The grounds of the villa have been one vast flowering field for some time now, with blooms and butterflies, and dogs chasing after shadows. Now, even the late-blossoming boulevards of the Prati quarter have changed and are suddenly garbed all in green. There, streets, houses, military barracks, and plane trees seem especially Piedmontese. They seem to extend, and make more distinct, each of the seasons. Even here, where seasons tend to merge one into the next without contrast, where winter displays the colours of March and all harshness, whether northern or southern, seems to halt, like an army of barbarians suddenly struck meek outside the city gates, never to pass within the great walls of Rome.[1]

The sudden transformation of trees, in the adolescent springtime of Turin, was always the most unexpected and deeply moving miracle of childhood. We would stay at home for a week during the Easter holidays, with a grey sky still nursing its wintry moods and trees standing black against that sky, stark trunks and branches, trellises, hieroglyphics of the cold. But when we went back to school, the world was another: each plant had sprouted feathers, fluffing up like a bird, swelling with a soul-stirring green. The plane trees had opened their thousands of little green hands; the horse chestnuts, yearning to light their chandeliers of flowers for the June insects, formed the green, endlessly shifting walls of my imagination. And further north, the metamorphosis is even more intimate and stirring. In Paris, where the air is so delicate that each colour glistens with the vibrancy of a Renoir, the first, shy spring leaves along the boulevards are like water emeralds on the damp black bark.

The larger the city, the harsher, the more alienating, and mechanical, life is there, and the more miraculous this vegetal truth appears. This rebirth and return to life have engendered mythologies and religions and our very sense of time, motion, order, and love. And so trees remain, amidst the asphalt, the innate binding force and loyal servants of the city at large, a living image of affectionate freedom.

That is why Herr Keuner[2] liked them too (Bertolt Brecht's mouthpiece, whose 'tales' can be read in the same volume that contains the translation of Brecht's novella *Die Geschäfte des Herrn Julius Caesar*).

> When asked about his relationship with nature, Herr K. replied: Sometimes, when I walk out of my house, I would be glad to see a tree or two. Especially because, by changing appearance according to the hour and the season, they attain a special degree of reality. Moreover, in the city, the unbroken panorama of useful objects – houses and streets that, if uninhabited, would appear empty and, if not used, have no meaning – in time scrambles our thoughts.

> Our particular social order causes us to consider human beings as useful objects as well, and so trees, at least for someone like me who is not a carpenter, therefore possess a degree of reassuring aloofness, indifferent to my existence. I would hope that even to carpenters, trees contain a certain something that defies usefulness.

In Rome, many things defy usefulness: perhaps that is why trees are not accorded much respect. But here, where nothing changes and bursts forth, not even the seasons, where not even nature allows revolutions, spring becomes at once forest and architecture, with the azalea festival on the Spanish Steps in April. This year, it seems lovelier than usual. It is lovely to behold at any hour of the day or night. The best time to see it is towards nightfall, from beneath, when the sky behind the church of Trinità dei Monti is already dark but still vaguely luminous. Between the backdrops of houses the grove of azaleas lining the steps is a murmuring waterfall of colours that finds, in the surrounding shadow, a small, harmonious, perfect scale of its own, appearing to be a living thing, glowing with an inner light. Or you may also pass by there when the sun is high in the sky, about two in the afternoon. At that hour, amidst tourists and idlers, the Piazza di Spagna, the boulevards of the Pincio, and all the surrounding streets are full of flocks of girls dressed in the white or colourful smocks they wear at work. It is the new thing this spring. Until this year, I had never run into them; they are the salesgirls and employees of clothing factories, shops, hairdressers, clinics, and dressmakers. Up until last year, when it was time for their lunch hour, they would take off their smocks, put on their lipstick, blend

Between the backdrops of houses the grove of azaleas lining the steps is a murmuring waterfall of colours that finds … glowing with an inner light.

in with the crowd, and disappear. This year, all of a sudden, they have changed their habits, appearing in the streets, as if they were walking into a house that they own. They look neither left nor right, they stroll in the bright sunshine, arm in arm, confident, serious, relaxed, and laughing with the attitude, in some sense, that they too are actors in the play. Before, they just weren't there: now they are emerging, proud of being workers, proud that they defy usefulness, that they are not instruments, wearing their work smocks like so many leaves, like plants in the springtime.

CHAPTER XVIII

A Dawn in Rome

For many years now, I have risen only rarely at dawn. When I do, apart from exceptional occasions, it is almost always when I am travelling somewhere and I need to take an early morning train. Then, that sense of the unaccustomed, the mysterious, and exotic that I find at this time of day, normally concealed and non-existent, sweeps me away to somewhere else, to a place and time far more distant than the destination to which the train will take me. The fresh lightness of the air, the silence, the colourless objects that seem on the verge of birth, all these things on their own give the heart a youthful sense of cheerful excitement (and perhaps, in a way, a sense of the sacred, as if one were entering a place inhabited by some unknown and inconceivably ancient god).

Rome, at this hour, which varies with the seasons, is enchantingly deserted: inhabited only by a populace of statues, stone animals, and architecture, which seem to be living their true, unseen lives in that astonished silent serenity. The street lights blink off, the stars wink out, the night has made its escape, surreal colours glow in the half-light, all is being readied for the light of reality.

If it is rare for me to rise at dawn, it is on the other hand quite common for me to arrive at dawn, as it were, from the other direction: after a night spent in some other pursuit. It is not idle play, but work, that pushes me to be like the Giovin Signore, or Young Master, described by Giuseppe Parini, who closes his eyes to the crowing of 'the cock, who is more accustomed to opening them for others'.[1] In the last few weeks, in order to finish a book about Germany, I have spent all, or nearly all, my nights, the only time that is proof against the distractions of the needy, the telephone, my friends, and the world at large, writing. This morning, having made corrections to the last few problematic passages, having reviewed the last commas, I finished my book and managed to submit it to the publisher at the last possible moment that would still allow it to be printed before the summer. This, then, was the last night of work. As it approached half past four in the morning, I walked out into the park, for a break from the monotony of hard work and words.

Rome, at this hour, which varies with the seasons, is enchantingly deserted: inhabited only by a populace of statues, stone animals, and architecture, which seem to be living their true, unseen lives in that astonished silent serenity.

The sky was already light: but my eyes, in the faint grey of the hour, composed of an opaque silver, as if hopefully wishing and waiting for the imminent arrival of colours, could see no further than the meadow and the trees that surround it. An unusual mist enveloped everything, sticky, moist, and dense, warm against the chilly shivers of the breeze. I looked out over the wall that looms high over the city and nothing met my eyes but that whitish mass, that smooth, concealing cloud. Only, in the far distance, like a slight and solemn phantom, could I make out the dome of St Peter's and the outline of Monte Mario, with the red lights of the pylons, against the opalescent sky.

The invisible city was silent: but in the grounds of the villa the air was filled, all around me, with a high-pitched and continuous music: thousands and thousands of birds were pouring out their song. Nearby, in the large leafy tree that blocked the sky from my sight, like a soloist at a concert, with phrases, warbles, chirps, laments, interruptions, trills, and variations, a nightingale was singing. Its free-form singing was supported and followed by the unbroken and many-voiced accompaniment of all sorts of lesser birds: sparrows, finches, blackbirds, starlings, each with its own language, with different intonations. I was quite familiar with these sweet melodies, these musical rapports orchestrated by the leafy branches, by the greenery, emerging from the vegetal slumber even before sunlight colours the day.

But, as I leant listening against the wall, from somewhere beneath me, from the vegetable patches that still survive, concealed behind the blocks of flats along the Via Flaminia, another song was rising in the air, mingling in a blend that was to me unusual, and extraordinary. It was the crowing of dozens and dozens of distant cocks, with their melancholy solitary glory, the piercing, triumphant lament, courageous and desolate, of the combed warriors, prisoners of the hen house.

I had never heard that metallic chorus and that woodland melody together. At the sound of that unprecedented wonder, my heart filled with the rare sensation of something new, of a discovery. 'How strange!' I murmured to myself. 'Together the cock and the nightingale sing!' I realized, as I spoke the words, that this observation was a hendecasyllabic line of verse: but, above all, it seemed to me that it possessed a meaning that went well beyond the occasion and the words.

These distant and diverse creatures were singing together: and all was one, in the short distance visible to my eyes, in the great space covered by fog. Everything fitted together. 'The sweetness of the world is one, one, one,' went the melody, and the chorus and the various voices melded, over the silence, into a shared song.

'Together the cock and the nightingale sing.' And for an instant it seemed to me as if I had discovered a hidden reality and had made my way, through love, into a true thing, that I was at the heart of things and that I was, with them, happy in spite of everything.

CHAPTER XIX

Summer Journey

This year, summer descended upon Rome, heavy, merciless, like an invisible object weighing everything down; as if the air had solidified and was pressing down upon men's shoulders, the way that age, medicine, or illness do: like a soldier's rucksack on a sweaty, endless march. Greyish mottled clouds gather in the sky, like sullen threats, only to vanish amidst the muggy breathlessness. Beneath the blazing sun, the lawns of the Villa Borghese wilt, as the green fades away; the soil turns to dust: scattered across that dust and the jaundiced blades of grass are the paper wrappings of yesterday's picnic lunches, crusts of dried bread covered by swarming ants. In the shade of mighty plane trees lie human bodies, like so many forgotten corpses; inevitably, a newspaper covers their face. The way they sleep is so stubborn, wilful, deliberate, headstrong, and unreserved, that it resembles death: there are some who, in a quest for greater coolness, have chosen to lie in a grassy depression, where the sun is also a little less fierce.

It is a broad meadow, set aside for dogs to ramble freely across, racing to and fro, sniffing delightedly at interesting scents, imagining distant and wild countryside, chasing after shadows, happy childhood illusions. Ah, how they wish they could be men, so that they could join the game, alongside the soldiers on leave, who are in turn delighted to have found a company of peers, kicking the football to and fro. The soldiers are surrounded by a crowd of little boys wearing colourful jerseys, as excited and questing as puppies towards these grown-ups in uniform, these farmhands embarrassed by their bodies and by the ball! Matrons and maids walk the dogs and chat beneath the trees. The dogs meet, sniff one another, exchange formal greetings, and establish friendships in accordance with their mysterious elective affinities, making a show of not hearing their names being called when the time comes to leave, so sweet is this Eden-like garden to their doggy sensibilities. 'Let us stay here just a little longer!' they seem to say. Then, once the case is clearly hopeless, they set off at a trot, looking backwards at each step.

The meadow is filled with tour groups from far away. The buses that conveyed them here sit parked along the boulevards, around the meadow, like giant cockroaches. They are mostly women, young and old and children, with a few men thrown in. They seem exhausted: they sit on the ground, they take off their shoes, they run their toes through the grass. Each tour group is accompanied by an accordion player. Rising into the still air are the plangent sound and the rapid beat of a tarantella: the girls dance, hand in hand, spinning intently, as if this were work, as if it were a duty. The others gather around, abandoning for a short time their frittata and cheese sandwiches, which they munch, exhausted and lazy, on the grass. The little girls have dark melancholy eyes, eyes that knew everything before beginning to see, eyes in which everything, before existing, had already become part of the past: the dark eyes of the south. The colourful outfits, the shape of their shoulders, their tiny sizes, round heads, long eyelashes, and the vaguely antique character of their poses and expressions, the natural way that they place their feet, and the sorrowful, shrewd patience of their faces, all show that they come from down there, from one of the villages of the Italian south.

Every weekday and holiday sees a procession of tour buses, bearing the same load of humanity and the same rural scenes of rest, dancing, picnics, exhaustion: and the lassitude of an adventure confined within the boundaries of the neighbourhood: mothers, aunts, godmothers, sons, and daughters. This is the sad and familiar tourism of an impoverished underclass, for whom even fun and amusement, and the miracle of a journey beyond the inviolable boundaries of poverty, still take the passive form of work and charity bestowed without a choice, whose natural price is a disquiet that is never discussed. Today, the tour buses come from Pozzuoli: these are tours organized by a few parish churches. They departed at three in the morning, wearing their Sunday best and high-heeled shoes; they were carsick. They arrived in Rome in time to attend Mass and spent the morning touring four or five little-known churches, selected not for their beauty or artistic interest, but because of some relic or other, or because of the name of the saint, male or female, to whom they are dedicated. Then they went to St Peter's as well; and then here, to this lawn, to have lunch, to rest, to kill time. In the afternoon they will go (unquestioningly, as if it were an obligation to which they were resigned) to Tivoli and then, without stopping over, in the evening, they will return home.

Rising into the still air are the plangent sound and the rapid beat of a tarantella: the girls dance, hand in hand, spinning intently, as if this were work, as if it were a duty.

This is the programme, identical for each of these journeys. They gather, alone, in the middle of the lawn, where not even the ice-cream van passes. From the nearby zoo, you can occasionally hear the lions roaring. The children do not seem curious about the sound. Their journey is an abstract movement, indifferent to places and things, through an empty land.

A little further along, in another section of the park, in the tiny puppet theatre, as on any other day, Pulcinella, or Punch, fierce, brave, and cowardly, performs his unchanging fable, nasal and ear-piercing. The children, different children, blond, soft, clean, and slender, watch him in amazed enchantment. What do they think of him, this folk Don Juan?[1] Before their gentle eyes, in duels fought with that plebeian weapon the cudgel, he kills all his entirely random enemies, one after the other, driven solely by an insatiable life force. Finally, the devil arrives, and he faces him too, insolent and heroic, with his club; and last of all comes death to bring down the curtain.

All around tourists slip by in their cars, an aeroplane glitters in the sunshine, the Saharan wind passes like the hot breath of a steam iron on your cheek. A cloud swells, darkens, spreads, threatens, and, in the bright light, dissolves.

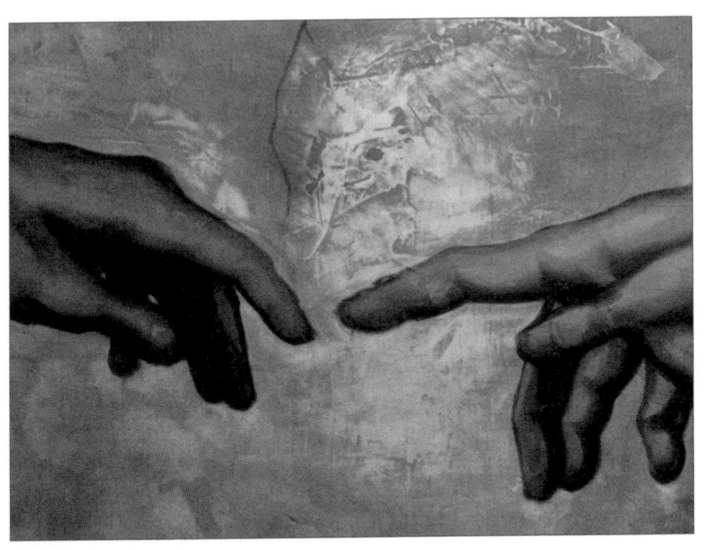

CHAPTER XX

The New Moon

Images slip rapidly by, vanishing into the shadows of memory, as, every day, new images overtake them, replacing them in an unbroken stream, like the compact, constantly replenished waters of a rushing, rapid river. But the images of the night of 13 September, when nothing actually happened that could be seen with the human eye, will not be concealed in the clouds of time. It was a deeply moving night of obscure emotions, more vague, profound, and dark than the fanciful sparkling of imagination.

We all looked at the moon: a three-quarter moon, crystal clear in the cloudless sky, with its shapes and its spots, where everyone over the centuries has imagined faces and thorns; with the dark zone on the right, where we thought we could see a crouching dog and that we later learned was called the Sea of Tranquillity, the Sea of Serenity, the Sea of Vapours. It was the cold white moon you see every night: but our wait made it seem different, as if this were the last time we were going to see it and it might suddenly disappear. Two young people, my niece and nephew, luminous in the freshness of their age, had brought along a pair of tiny opera glasses. They brought the moon only a little closer and distorted the colours of the outline; but we each clamoured to look through them as if they could unveil a mystery hidden to the naked eye. The older girl, Amelia, told us that she had dreamed of a pious maiden, her blonde head draped in an ecclesiastic veil, who said to her, 'Tomorrow, the Virgin of Fatima will descend from the sky, by helicopter. Let us go and wait for her together. Pay no attention to the moon. The moon is a thin, fragile globe, empty inside. If the rocket hits it, it may punch right through it, and through the hole you will be able to see the dark sky. Or maybe it will shatter into a thousand pieces, or into dust. There are so many lovely things on earth: why worry about the moon?' That dream reminded the young people of Leopardi's dream:

> Hark, Melisso: I want to tell you of a dream
> I had this night, which comes back to me
> As I glimpse the moon...

the dream of Alceta, in which he saw the moon fall into the middle of a meadow, and in that piece of sky from which the moon had broken away, there remained a glimmer, or a niche. And they worked to reconstruct, from their memories and with my help, that sublime fragment, that mysterious, nocturnal dialogue between shepherds, to the very end:

> ...but there is only
> This moon in the heavens, and no one
> Has ever seen it fall, save in a dream.[1]

We knew that we would not be able to see anything: but our dreams brought us out all the same. When the long-awaited hour drew near, the moon seemed to wreathe herself in a luminous, colourful halo that soon vanished, perhaps nothing more than a faint and fast-moving cloud, but which seemed like the moon's response to those who had touched her for the first time ever. All around us, everyone was looking into the sky, with various expressions and emotions. Some stood in silence, others joked aloud, some applauded, and there were those who did not want to look, as if frightened by this new world of movement and clamour, so dear to the hearts of others. There were those who felt they were proud participants in what could be considered the greatest piece of sharpshooting of all time. A kind lady sympathized with the moon, no longer inviolate, noble and solitary, an inaccessible virgin queen, and spoke to her in a comforting tone, trying to console her. Another woman sang, in a lovely silvery lunar voice, 'Casta diva'.[2] Everyone reacted in some particular manner, each in accordance with their character and nature. Then we heard the voice of Radio Moscow announcing, in French, that the rocket had reached the moon: and, immediately thereafter, the cheerful notes of a series of popular songs, which echoed out, as stirring as a 'Marseillaise' from the sky.

The moon rode in the sky, a little closer, a little more pitiable. The youngsters, tired out from the day's activities, nodded sleepily.

In the velvety air of the Roman night, we imagined a distant square crowded with people, excited, happy, triumphant. Here, some were raising toasts, while others seemed upset, as if they had witnessed a sacrilege; while others spoke of the manly gesture, of this reaching beyond ourselves, this disinterested attainment of an 'other' and an 'elsewhere', as a decisive development for the souls of men. What mattered to them was not the pride of power, nor was it the science (much less the escapism, whether fantastic or real, the return to a boundless childhood). On the contrary, it was this new capacity to contact things, taken to the furthermost extreme: to establish contact with the eternal symbol of untouchable solitude. And it appeared, far more profound than the various considerations of the moment, that this was to one and all the signal of a beginning, a new time, a new mythology, a new poetic possibility. The signal of the fall of a boundary, natural and arbitrary; and of the end of the crisis of detachment, separation, inability to communicate, and anguish. That invisible gesture, that object, that symbol fallen into an arid, dusty desert, from what depths, prior to reason itself, did it touch in our hearts the very roots of emotion? Certainly, a loving sense of liberty seems to envelop all possibilities.

The moon rode in the sky, a little closer, a little more pitiable. The youngsters, tired out from the day's activities, nodded sleepily.

CHAPTER XXI

San Lorenzo and San Paolo

The summer weighs down upon us, with heat-yellowed clouds louring in the oppressive sky, only to be dragged away and scattered by a high wind from Africa: then, suddenly, the air currents shift and an unexpected coolness arrives, like a vital contradiction. Rome lies, sunlit, festooned with flags, shattered, transformed into a labyrinth without a thread, beneath these shifting gusts of wind, awaiting the Olympics and the people of every colour who will soon arrive: perhaps, actually, expecting nothing, with no real curiosity about the impending multicolour invasion. In her streets, impassable and obligatory, it seems that Rome is readying herself, without any real changes, as she does every year, for the deserted solitude of the holidays, and yet we might say that something deep within her has changed: an interest, a hope, an inner movement.

More than ever before, life is taking place on two simultaneous and very distant planes: one is apparent, a plane of indifference, confident of the eternity of time, satisfied with the everyday, scornful of the different that claims to be new. The other plane is hidden, one of deep-rooted human emotions, dignity, and unassuming pride. The young people of Porta San Paolo don't show themselves much, but you can sense their presence and, as in the rest of Italy, here too people understand that something, with the events of July [in these recent times],[1] has changed. A new confidence appears on the faces of the common folk, a greater vitality animates their gestures and enlivens their gazes, and passions well to the surface that no longer seem useless or impossible. If Stendhal could be here now, in Rome, he would notice these new passions with delight and he would rightly say that boredom has vanished. Certainly boredom, Roman boredom, as compact and impenetrable as the ancient city walls, barely nicked by time and moss, along which lizards run, the boredom that nests in foreheads smoothed out by the shadow of tight, raven-black curls, the age-old boredom described by Moravia, adolescent and domestic, was crushed underfoot and destroyed by charging mounted *carabinieri*[2] [there, just where the Germans also met with resistance, at Porta San Paolo]. Through the breach ripped open in the traditional walls of boredom, here too, young people have escaped, actively committed to change and free self-affirmation, invisible masters of the empty city. This modification, this change in attitude in a city that is accustomed to devouring changes, gulping them down impassively, even seems to be reflected in the weather and the season, in the rapid shifts from muggy heat to cool and refreshing western breezes, in spring-like clearings of the leaden overcast. These are the nights of falling stars. Among the trees behind the villa, I scrutinize the sky patiently, to see if some star goes hurtling across it, only to disappear. But the sky is dense with haze, and the luminous moon shines on that translucent screen, whitening it and hiding the stars from my gaze. What holds me here now peering in vain into that lofty, miserly sky, if not an image from my childhood? That forbidden, enchanted hour of the night, that lovely, ineffable mystery of elusive meteors, that exquisite anguish of infinity. And, at the same time, the voices of the nannies, those solid representatives of the outside world, with their boundless and

These are the nights of falling stars. Among the trees behind the villa, I scrutinize the sky patiently, to see if some star goes hurtling across it, only to disappear. But the sky is dense with haze, and the luminous moon shines on that translucent screen, whitening it and hiding the stars from my gaze.

persuasive authority, in the closed domestic paradise, who made those stars into repositories of hope and desire. So, each year, stargazing remained a needful ritual, and has preserved its ability to produce a touch of poetry, intact, ever since those distant times. Contaminated only, alas, by a literary memory, it too as ancient as the first years of school, and it too recurring awkwardly and mixing with the lovely celestial response, because even then it stuck in the mind like something that didn't belong, sticking fast, resisting expulsion, no matter how hard I might try to cast it out and, at the same time, with an unpleasant sound of fakery which I could never quite pin down. The memory was of the first four lines of a poem by Pascoli. Every Italian knows them by heart:

> San Lorenzo, I know why such a multitude
> Of stars, through the still air
> Burns and falls, why such great weeping
> In the concave vault glitters.[3]

The memory went no further, the rest of the poem was cancelled each time, perhaps because even then, with a child's natural instinct for self-defence, it was natural to cancel and reject baby birds, dollies, atrocities, and saccharine imagery of every kind.

And now I was looking at the sky again: no stars fell. Why did I continue to hear an error, a falsehood in those lovely lines of verse? Why did that *pianto* 'weeping' (which obliges us, in order to keep the rhyme, to say *tanto di stelle* 'such a multitude of stars' instead of *tante stelle* 'so many stars') seem false, emphasized at the end of the verse, that weeping that 'glitters', that weeping in the 'concave' sky? And yet the poet's real emotion must necessarily have been deep-seated and heartfelt: it was the fundamental emotion of his life: his grief over his father's murder. But the image always lies either above or below the truth, as if the intensity of the trauma could never attain direct expression, wavering between a puny and cliché-ridden sentimentality and the cosmic diction of the worlds, spangling with stellar tears 'this opaque atom of evil'. The poet happened to replace the reality of emotion with the taste for emotion, interpreting and obeying, or perhaps foreshadowing, the trend of his time. And so, I could not help but think of Umberto Saba's admirable and youthful essay 'Quello che resta da fare ai poeti' ('What Remains to be Done by Poets'). Not only is it a jewel of the printer's art, with its magnificent typeface from the Zibaldone press, but it is also a fine piece of analysis, a clear and manly way to conceive of poetry and life, which is perhaps more valuable and instructive today than it was even in 1911, when it was written. How perceptive Saba is in examining and finding errors in certain of his verses and assigning to poetry the duty of moral clarity, honesty!

Of course, poetry is an expression of an individual world, which it makes valid for everyone else. 'What remains to be done by poets is to write honest poetry,' says Saba. His voice is meant, now more than ever, for young people, and they understand him. It is in this direction that what seems new today is moving, and it concerns non-poets as well as poets.

Among the new young people, emerging now from the darkness of the piazza, there were certainly non-poets and poets, together. [But for both the former and the latter, whether they turn to the heaven of San Lorenzo or that of San Paolo, the stars do not weep. I look into the sky, at the absent falling stars: and I see a light passing, in luminous flight, the Echo of the Earth.] [Think of 25 August.]

At Porta San Paolo there were certainly both non-poets and poets together. San Lorenzo and San Paolo, or St Lawrence and St Paul, are not far away, on their thrones, in the heaven of stars.

CHAPTER XXII

A Child in Flight

Beneath the ageing sun of summer, the age-old face of Rome has changed as well. Festive banners flutter in the wind, along with the insignia, or the heraldic crests, the devices, the stripes, the stars, the sickles, the hammers, the suns, the crescent moons, the colours of every nation. A population of athletes settles in, some of them spectacularly beautiful – harmonious and serene champions – many of them however quite ordinary in appearance, resembling people you would meet every day. Others are in some way or other conditioned in their form for the activities at which they excel, bodies smooth as fish, round heads, bull necks or turtle necks, butterflies, grasshoppers, giraffes, giants, and dwarves; glistening faces, calm faces, or nervous, tense faces; blue eyes and black eyes; shapes from every land; just the way they are, big and small, proud and modest, the finest on earth.

Everything has been said, in the past few days, about the Olympics: the good and the bad, the glories and the speculations, the values and the empty phrases, athletic excellence and crass moneymaking, peace and rhetoric. But this diverse and strong-limbed people that passed through here, what has it left behind for us? A number of images that stir our hearts and our imaginations: the physical and visible appearance of happiness.

Happiness, a great and unsullied happiness: the immediate sense of blood pumping through the arteries, of muscles swelling with joyous, natural strength, of breath sweeping like a breeze and tossing the leaves of a forest, of limitless power: a song, a flight: the childhood dream of levitation, of moving weightless through the air, rowing, free of all heaviness, a dream become reality.

In the middle of the broad green field, populated with colours, lines, yellow lanes, a festive air, in the centre of the ring of people crowding the stands, is a black girl, tall, slender, graceful in her dark-blue tracksuit. She is Wilma Rudolph, the fastest of all, a natural. How happy she is, standing there alone! I watch her as she moves delicately, as if performing the steps of a dance, wearing a colourful straw hat, worn playfully, charmingly; the distracted, gloriously modest demeanour of a child triumphant at being a child. She listens to her gestures and takes pleasure from them, like a black Natalia Rostov,[1] who sits shut up in her room, listening to herself as she sings, suddenly brimming over, as she hears herself, with the ineffable happiness of youth. She is entirely self-contained, taken up with her ceaseless play, her twenty years of age that have never encountered the useless outside world, in her candid corporeal beatitude, sufficient unto herself. But when the race begins, oh, then she's the blink of an eye, an animal uncaged, she is an angel, and she takes flight.

She is entirely self-contained, taken up with her ceaseless play, her twenty years of age that have never encountered the useless outside world, in her candid corporeal beatitude, sufficient unto herself. But when the race begins, oh, then she's the blink of an eye, an animal uncaged, she is an angel, and she takes flight.

Then, where is her house, too small for the sixteen brothers and sisters, in Tennessee, where is the university and the burden of everyday problems, the soul-killing prejudice of colour? On the green field, her colour is the loveliest of them all. She wins, she is loved and admired: evil is banished.

(Only if you beat everyone, only if you are first, can you be fully happy, without restrictions or effort, like a king: then you are a king, then there is no one ahead of you. Already the happiness of second place consists of effort and exhaustion.)

The same airy happiness in flight, feather-light, without a shadow, can be found in Livio Berruti. He is a polite young man; rarely will you find anyone who is more of the perfect 'Turinese', serious, clear-eyed, modest, not particularly athletic in appearance. I sense that he is not a cold person, as the ignorant like to say of him, based on preconceptions: certainly, he feels within himself that ineffable power. He wears glasses, even when he runs and his gestures have the refined delicacy of the intellectual (like the Russian champion of the triple jump, who resembles him).Those hand gestures suggest that the internal power that makes a champion is really no different from that which prepares an artist or a great man of culture, in their youthful years, years of unlimited power. (Piero Gobetti had it, this smiling image of youth. 'You are the living example of what Nietzsche said, that true courage smiles,' Umberto Saba wrote to him in 1922. He could outrace us all, in the Piazza Castello, during the intervals of the tetralogies at the Teatro Regio, Turin's Royal Theatre. Oh, we never timed those races: but certainly that inner power that made him first amongst us had the same nature as the power that expressed itself in his life and thought.)

Berruti, how he appeals to us, as if via an ancient memory, how easy it is to grasp his every flying act and gesture! There exists, I was thinking to myself, as I watched him in the moment of victory, a language of gestures, an expressive way of moving: and it is as different as the spoken language in various countries. This language was especially visible in the stances and poses of the boxers. In the vast round basin of the Palazzo dello Sport, beneath Nervi's magnificent dome, young men from every nation assailed each other. Of course, neither I nor the friends who were there with me are nationalists. Indeed, certain of my friends are so morally offended by the vulgar sentimentality, the quavering rhetoric of the announcers, that by reaction, they tend to root for non-Italians, as they are unable to abide the unseemly tradition of Fascist conceit, arrogant in victory, and whining and defensive in defeat. All the same, I point out to them, and they were forced to concede, that the Italians appeared to us to be better than all the others. I would venture to say that nearly all of them were really first-rate (and not just as boxers, but as people, such as the young, blond Bossi, for instance, a Milanese, sportsmanlike and cheerful, even in defeat). And they seemed to us to be the best, even when they weren't; and even when we could clearly see that they weren't the best, our opinion remained the same. Why? Perhaps only because we understood every one of their gestures and emotions better than we did those of the others, as well as their fears, their hesitations, their missteps, and we recognized them as our own; we knew every detail, every nuance of their movements, we knew what they meant.

I believe that this understanding of a language of gestures, this love of one's own image (to quote a phrase of Rocco Scotellaro's),[2] is the chief cause of spontaneous partisanship, the good and necessary part of it. (Overlapping it, a negative factor, is false pride in one's city, one's nation.) These two dynamics taken together (but the former, more than the latter) are the reason that applause bursts out by group: the Czechoslovakians, the French, the tenacious, proud Poles, the Americans; and especially, numerous and wildly enthusiastic, the Germans, who, amidst the cheering on the field, come together at a run, embracing festively, East Germans and West Germans.

This recognition of one's own language in gestures, in actions, in styles, encourages and creates the process of identification. With 'our boys and girls' that identification is immediate, instinctive, a product of shared experience. It occurs with 'others' as well and when it does it sometimes takes place at a deeper level. Why was Wilma Rudolph, a young black girl, looked upon by a hundred thousand pairs of eyes with a sense of kinship? Wilma Rudolph took everyone back to an absolute childhood, the joy of having a body: such a primordial feeling that we all identify with her, her black skin is of no importance: a child in flight, a feather-light angel (what we all wish we could have been, what we all, at some point – perhaps when we ran to our mother, the first pure source of delight – have been). Everyone cheered for her, for her celestial grace: because she restored to each of us our lost power, the limitless time of childhood, the inner certainty of existence.

(That certainty, once we leave the stadium, vanishes. We enter a maze, an unrecognizable city, where the familiar places have become, by some evil spell, different and unattainable, where distances have shifted in the continual and obligatory turning upon one's heel. Where a strange forest of street signs give the unpleasant sensation of an alien, primitive jungle and one despairs of finding oneself in a non-place, whose size and way is no longer familiar, a way that has become forbidden. In place of the way, we find a sense of play, which here shows its absurd side.)

It is all play, but frequently it possesses the profound truth that is often present in play. We speak of the value of peace in the shared life of the athletes, and it is true. In an upmarket restaurant in the centre of Rome, I see three athletes, who have escaped their village to see the town. They speak English: they are three world champions: a white American, a black American, a Soviet. They are all equally tall and very tall indeed; they all have the same honest appearance, they are three brothers. A foolish sheep of an autograph hunter approaches them. They sign his little cards with their names and nations. The fool cannot believe, given the athlete's spoken English and the fool's prejudice, that the Soviet, so clearly a friend of the other two, could really be a Russian. 'You're kidding!' he says. The Russian insists, then, grasping the cunning and impenetrably closed mind of the man to whom he is speaking, tells him playfully (the way you talk to crazy people, to humour them), 'Of course, of course, don't worry. Can't you see that I am South African?' and he laughs with his two friends at the foolish sheep's satisfaction, then walks off, arm in arm with his friends, with the white man and the black man.

The games are over. Rome has played at transforming itself (this city that never plays, that is never childish) into something else: now it returns to its everyday weight, the weight of things that descend from their free heaven and stop, becoming motionless, burdensome stone, full of impassive history.

CHAPTER XXIII

After the Party

So, the Olympics are over and Rome too goes back to everyday life, like all the cities and villages and the countryside, where there never was, where there never is a holiday from work and from need. The games were a lovely spectacle from every point of view: the colours of peace, flags, strength, youth, the fascinating measurement of power at the limits of human potential. They were such a wonderful show that even the impenetrable, elderly Romans, these armoured tortoises, these lizards basking on their time-encrusted walls, wound up taking an interest. One of these old men was saying, in the local cafe, on the first day, as the games were beginning, 'That torch, I mean, that torch, what is that? I wish I was Nero, and that I had a thousand torches, I'd light every last one and burn everything to the ground.' But another old man answered him promptly, pointing out that the torch had made him 'feel a certain something right here', when he saw those young people 'running as fast as ten kilometres per hour' and handing the torch one to another, along the Corso, going like the wind. In the end, these ancient, post-historical human lizards were satisfied, because they had seen an Abyssinian (things happen for a reason) win the marathon running barefoot, beneath the Arch of Constantine, right at the entrance to the Via dell'Impero, not far from the obelisk of Aksum.[1] This seemed to correspond, in a certain sense, to that supreme and natural form of justice that, provided you are patient, will eventually out. The Olympics had become likeable. They culminated in the final spectacular burst of fireworks in all the neighbourhoods on the far side of the river Tiber. The Japanese fireworks, at Castel Sant'Angelo, were the least popular, because they weren't very noisy and they never changed, nothing but globes and suns in various colours, as in the Japanese flag, and not varied and brilliant and thunderous, like the fireworks made by Coccia from Paliano, the best firework-maker on earth. How lovely, Rome illuminated, showered in fire! From a very high terrace, in the cold Tramontane wind, you could see the city spread out below, embraced by that festive light, with the architecture of all the various different times, with its parallel, simultaneous lives, its splendours and its contradictions. Then, the last bomb sailed up into the sky, the last explosion thundered out, and the velvety dark of night returned, lit from afar by the bursts of flame from the trees and scrub on Monte Mario, ignited by the devices of the pyrotechnists, and fanned by the night winds.

The party was over, the interval concluded. Everything had gone well, the records had all been beaten, even the Italians had put on a good show. The little boys in the parks and on the playing fields performed leaps and ran races in keeping with Olympic regulations, and television had proved that it can be an interesting and exceedingly useful medium if it restricts itself, as it should, to portraying actual events.

Life as usual was beginning again, after the spectacular burst of fireworks, with different faces and different appearances. Already, the next day, at Monte Mario, the cornerstone was being laid for the much-discussed Hilton hotel. 'We can reduce to the bare essentials', read the newspaper account that appeared in *Il messaggero*, 'our report on the ceremony yesterday that inaugurated yet another irreparable insult to the city. On the empty site where the hotel will one day stand, the mayor of Rome, Cioccetti, greeted the chairman of the property developer, otherwise the engineer Gualdi, to whom Rome owes no special debt of gratitude, the chairman of the Hilton Hotels Corporation, and Ambassador Zellerbach. Also present was the Italian minister for tourism, Filchi, whose speech hailed the construction of this new hotel as a sign of economic cooperation between Italy and the US, and evoked the long-ago era of assistance from the ERP (European Recovery Programme). Everything and everyone was given benediction by Cardinal Micara.' In short, they were all present: along with foreign businessmen and business-oriented politicos, all the true representatives of the other Italy, the Italy of *luigini*, or political lackeys, the Italy that lives on top and, shameless and careless, spins its web of privilege and self-interest.

The question of the Hilton hotel had been a long internecine battle, lost, after many twists and turns, in the face of a coalition of the most powerful interests. It had looked, for a while, as if it would be possible to keep this colossal hotel from defacing and defiling what survives of the already thoroughly defaced and defiled Monte Mario. These Hiltons seem to be colonial hotels, hotels that are about more than business, hotels that have to do with prestige and the cold war. They spring up in places where the goal is to establish a sense of power, such as Baghdad, Cairo, Havana, and Berlin, in countries where it was possible and desirable, when they were built, to create a foothold and a marker of ownership. That is what I was told in Berlin, which has its own absurd Hilton, built from billions (it cost 4 billion lire), as I describe in my book *La doppia notte dei tigli* (*The Two-Fold Night* or *The Linden Trees*). In the lobby of the hotel, with its exquisite leather floor, my Berliner friends who, in keeping with tradition, are determined to be witty at all costs, told me the bon mots that have sprung up about this latest propaganda creation: that is to say, that wherever these hotels are built, a war or a revolution breaks out immediately afterwards. Linking the inauguration of the hotel with the dangerous tension of the time, they congratulated me and all Italians for the fact that Rome, as it seemed at the time, had successfully refused permission to build upon its land (free and sacred, they said) so ill-omened a structure, a building that was such a bellwether of mighty storms to come.

Now, instead, we will have our Hilton – and we will also have our storms: and how could they not lash down upon us, since they are the natural product of dishonest government.

From up there, from Monte Mario, you can see the entire area that, by taking advantage of the Olympics to scramble the regulatory plan, has been handed over to speculators: the landholdings of the developer and various religious congregations, valued at Lord only knows how many billions of lire (as *ABC* and other publications have shown, with thorough and courageous investigative reports). You can see the Via Olimpica, which, however handsome it may be in itself with some excellent pieces of construction, such as the viaduct designed and built by Nervi, will only contribute to the progressive destruction of Rome. It is, in the words of Bruno Zevi,[2] (words that bear out the views of Luigi Piccinato[3] and other urban planners, who have been waging a battle in favour of the regulatory plan), 'the arbitrary grafting of a sector plan on to a wholly unplanned city', and will in reality be helpful to no one at all except for the specific landowners, already readying construction that will be profitable for them but ruinous to the city. These architects, correctly, see the loss of the values of the 'citizen', first with Fascism and now, the reason for the impossibility of any social order, and for the 'form' that such an order would take, namely the city.

From up there I can see again the Olympic Village, so alive when it was inhabited by young athletes, when men and women from every nation lived there together in peace. Architecturally it is not particularly attractive, the way the Palazzo dello Sport and the Palazzetto and the Velodrome and the Viaduct are. Now it is deserted, and slightly ghastly: and it already suggests its future monotonous bureaucratic use. An illustrated pamphlet about the village, which is above all a lyrical exaltation of the fatherly minister Togni (here I make only a passing reference to it, but it would be appropriate to explore it in greater detail at some later point), praises the kind of social diversity that will be attained here, with state employees of every level. It is certainly a good thing that so many families of valued public servants should have a decent home here (we would prefer not to let our thoughts wander to the possible political criteria involved in assigning those homes). And yet other uses might have seemed equally appropriate. A poet, Elsa Morante, imagined the village as a university campus: that is something we lack, just as we lack a genuine, living university. And perhaps, if a city of students were mingled here, without divisions, with some of the families of the poor and the unemployed from the great belt of the *borgate*, or poverty-stricken peripheral quarters, and some of the families of civil servants, it might create a non-artificial neighbourhood, full of human contacts, reciprocal experience, potential for enrichment, and understanding. These are nothing more than poetic dreams, unrealizable in the tawdry imaginations of bureaucrats.

... the Olympic Village, so alive when it was inhabited by young athletes, when men and women from every nation lived there together in peace.

From up there, from the summit of Monte Mario, which will be, from today onwards, off-limits to the people of the city, reserved only for passing millionaires, it seems as if you can see, for the last time, all Rome and all Italy together; and it seems that the constant and dramatic and true sound of life reaches all the way up here, the sound of intentions and needs and hopes. And you can sense (you can see) the enemy power that evicts and rejects humanity. It is right for them to protest and battle fearlessly. (If only they were all as daring as the 121 French men of culture who signed the Manifesto.) Because the solution to these problems – which concern not merely a city, but all cities and all the occurrences of everyday life for all of us – is not a technical solution, nor is it merely an urban solution, in the narrowest sense of the word. Rather it is a question of the existence of the state, of real power, of courage. This is one of the testing points for civic values in our country and a sense of internal freedom. Scornfully, they build Great Hotels. And they prepare, in these gentle breezes, the necessary and mighty storms.

CHAPTER XXIV

Substance and Chance

There are things on earth that appear wonderful, all the more so in that they are distant from our usual experience; and which, through coincidence, or permanence, and juxtapositions that are as evident as they are unpredictable, clearly reveal the truth. Last Friday, I had spent most of the afternoon immersed in the writings of Stendhal, engaged as I was in completing to a deadline the preface to a translation of *Rome, Naples et Florence.*[1] When I left my house, I was filled with the mind and soul of those stunning observations on Italy, of the images of a land he loved so well, a land of passion, sublime energy, and pure nature, beneath the extraneous crust of the past, this fatherland of his and ours, of genuine living men and anachronistic governments. I happened to find myself in the Piazza del Popolo (in the piazza that Stendhal so disliked) as the last in a series of political speeches was being delivered: and I found myself, as if by a miracle, physically enveloped in his world of 150 years ago.

There was already something about the crowd (which had been conveyed from small outlying towns in a great number of buses – I noticed one marked number 152) that was singularly obsolete, strange. It was not a crowd of lively, modern, active people, full of interests, hopes, initiatives, and thoughts for the future, such as you meet everywhere, in workplaces, in the countryside, in the streets, and which everywhere moves and expresses itself. Rather it was a collection of expressionless faces, with eyes that were at once patient, humble, and fanatical, which I could easily imagine as similar in character to the eyes of the 'common folk' of 1817, entirely devoid of 'civilization', and for whom, according to Stendhal, the words of Metternich were true ('a barbarous opinion, if you like'), that is, 'for them the rule of opinion or of the two chambers is not a "real need."' In those dim faces, it was clear that what was going on was not a discussion of ideas, nor a method for making choices, but rather a celebration, or an act of faithless idolatry, a practical, ritual ceremony. But the most remarkable thing, the thing that filled me with genuine admiration, was the words that were emanating from the podium.

In those dim faces, it was clear that what was going on was not a discussion of ideas, nor a method for making choices, but rather a celebration, or an act of faithless idolatry …

The orator who was speaking alternated a common parlance ('this joke of a left wing!' and so forth), with a singular, acute, perfect, and even rarefied, diction; with the distinguished voice and the *romanesco* refinement of my friend Rossellini. And, with supreme skill, he explored, on an ethereal plane, all imaginable issues, with an expert and original focus that was all his own. This speaker, clearly the most significant personality of those I know in his party, was the cabinet minister Andreotti.

Whether it was the singular audience from a bygone century that surrounded me in the piazza, whether it was the reading and the thoughts that had filled my day, whatever the reason, I could not help but identify him with one of Stendhal's many characters, with one of the characters from Stendhal's world of the Restoration, filled with the chilly passion of political calculation, and with that pessimism and fundamental scorn for humanity that is the source of an apparent clarity and confidence in action. He talked about everything: democracy and freedom, statistical satisfaction and human dissatisfaction, he attacked 'false men of culture', he said that the 'great success of our young Olympic champions had done much to debunk the myth of a spineless youth, rendered cretinous by fifteen years of Christian Democratic rule. We prefer the young people of the Olympics to the young people, so dear to the Communists, of *Rocco e dei suoi fratelli* (*Rocco and His Brothers*)'[2] (that Rocco who, alas, is an Olympic champion in the film). He praised the only effective internationalism, that of the three great men of Europe: Schuman, Adenauer, and De Gasperi. He played the nationalist card against Austria, and pan-Germanism, the Germany that has, he said, a two-fold nature, the positive side of science, technology, and art, the Germany of Adenauer, and the negative side, one element of which was Nazism. Just as the positive Germany had covered itself in glory, so had the negative Germany stained itself with crimes. But he added that it was necessary to distinguish between the 'chance' crime of the concentration camps and the substantial and cultural crime of the German (he was sufficiently refined to refrain from saying, as is customary, the Jew), the German Karl Marx. His use of the term 'chance' was perfect. There is a complete theory of crime and sin in this distinction.

The concentration camps were chance accidents of history, venial and atonable sins that, therefore, in absolute terms, do not count and do not exist: *Das Kapital* is a substantial, mortal, unforgivable sin: a manifestation and the incarnation of the devil.

In this singular, refined, theological style of oratory, the devil makes his appearance, with horns, tail, and mischief. We were truly once again in the presence of the illuminations of Stendhal, back in 1817; we were looking at ritual replacing politics. 'It is not the actions, of greater or lesser utility to men, but the scrupulous performance of rituals that, in this land, leads one to eternal happiness. An Italian feels and believes that you become happy in this world by satisfying one's passions and in the next life by having satisfied rituals. Mendicant monks educate the conscience of the common populace, where the lackeys and butlers are found, who in turn educate the conscience of the nobles.'

In the new world of the present day, these distinctions between the substantial and the fortuitous, these 'chance' concentration camps, were enough to suggest that even a technically free act of the popular will corresponds only in part to the reality of political passions and interests, and that in a country in motion, full of new developments and possibilities, the shifts in electoral numbers would be relatively slight.

There is a great inert mass, unconnected to culture and to life, for which the two chambers of the Italian parliament are not a 'real need', and do not really exist: for whom even voting has been transformed into a rite, into a form of obedience. If it were possible to remove from the voting results the votes of the civic committees, then the elections would be clear and would correspond to that which is real and alive in our country, both on the left and in the centre and on the right.

The charge that the Italian people have only a limited political awareness is just as baseless as the charge that is commonly repeated in the field of culture, namely that the Italians do not read, according to the figures for book sales. If we subtract from those numbers the people who simply cannot read, either because they have no money to buy books, or are too exhausted from working, then we will see that in Italy, in proportion to the possible readers, the actual readers are perhaps greater in number than in the countries with whom we usually compare ourselves. If, similarly, we exclude from our electoral calculations those who do not understand the state, because they are concerned solely with the afterlife, or out of ritual obedience (the political illiterates), or those who are not free, or do not feel free, for economic reasons, an analysis of electoral results would be equally encouraging and positive. But because this amorphous mass does exist, we must take account of it and understand that the methods of parliamentary election are not enough on their own. Alongside them, other forms of action, organization and political struggle are necessary in order to solve the nation's fundamental problems, to allow this country to walk and speak openly, without fearing the devil.

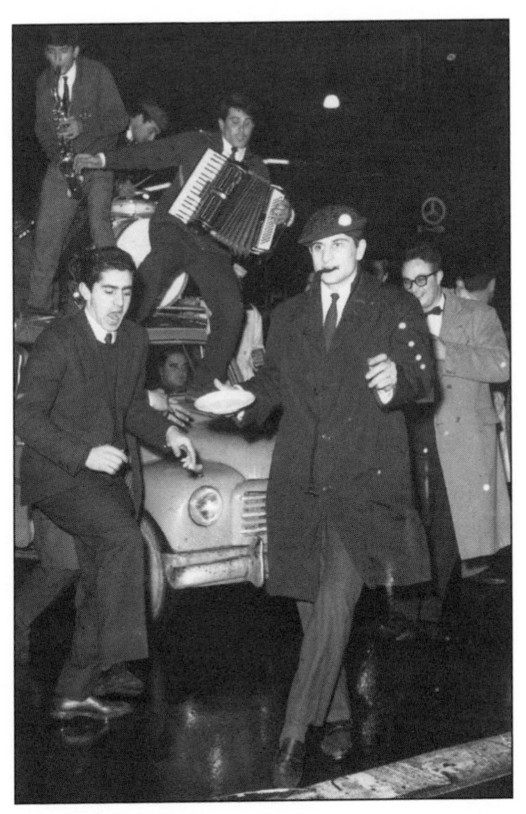

CHAPTER XXV

Clothes Moths

Nowhere else on earth but Rome, I think, are so many objects tossed out of windows, over balcony railings, off roofs at the end of the year, and these objects, shattering as they hit the street paving, symbolize evil, indeed the greatest of evils: time. They aren't tossed with the impersonal ritual routine of other cities, instead they are hurled with a sort of immediate ferocity, almost a gust of personal violence. It is not entirely clear whether that violence is directed against the very objects being thrown, or the ground upon which they plummet, or a set of unknown imaginary enemies that imagination sees populating the streets, or against the very act of hurling them, or even against oneself. Or (perhaps because the objects that are selected for tossing are no longer new and already bear the marks of time, cracked dishes, chipped drinking glasses, empty bottles, worm-eaten furniture: all objects that are, at least in part, already dead, or old, which must, like old people, fathers and mothers in certain savage tribes, be tossed off a roof) with a ferocity that certainly springs from a magic form of love.

Perhaps the Romans, in this New Year ceremony, are committing the initiatory ritual of killing father and mother, in order to ready for themselves a year of total liberty, a liberty that will gradually wane as the end of the year draws closer. Not only because of the numerous, multiform, and encroaching presence of all the fathers, possible, real, and symbolic, personified and dressed as mothers, but also because of the speed with which new things become adult and, soon thereafter decrepit, and can therefore immediately be tossed from the roof, only to start over again.

A friend of mine, whom I ran into late the other night as he was out walking with his wife, was imparting these thoughts to me, after the pelting rain of objects had obliged the two of them to take shelter under a balcony, their bodies pressed desperately against the wall. Now the three of us were walking along together, crushing underfoot broken glass, bottles, pieces of wood, crumpled paper, boxes, light bulbs, wicker baskets, bric-a-brac, rags, and every sort of clutter and rubbish that had rained down from above. And my friend went on, as if thinking aloud, or speaking about these domestic considerations to his wife, saying that this is the magical reason why it is rare, in Rome, to find anyone who keeps an outfit in perfect repair, or the furniture in their home, the accessories and furnishings, the linen, the bedclothes. There is no other city with a temperate climate and civilized customs on this earth in which clothes moths find so hospitable a terrain in which to flourish, feed, and multiply. A tattered wool sweater or a torn suit will not be mended or stitched; it will simply be thrown away, or given to the poor. This observation of a common state of affairs – he said – can be explained, not only by the magical and ritual reasons described above, but also with an historical and social interpretation.

There is no other city with a temperate climate and civilized customs on this earth in which clothes moths find so hospitable a terrain in which to flourish, feed, and multiply. A tattered wool sweater or a torn suit will not be mended or stitched; it will simply be thrown away, or given to the poor.

Despite the continual attraction of new inhabitants and the continual changes in the population at large, Rome does not possess, nor has it ever possessed – my friend observed – a genuine populace. That is to say, a middle class in its positive phase, rich in its own traditional virtues: an economic sense, the instinct for progressive, family-based creation, the pleasure and the glory of saving: a venerable bourgeoisie wholly bent on the early phase of capitalist accumulation. Rome has remained substantially comprised of aristocrats and paupers (with the addition of that peculiar aristocracy made up of paupers without heirs, the clergy). Now, why should an aristocrat take care of a suit? Why seek out someone to take care of it when he, by definition, can have all the suits he cares to; and when, to change them, to have them altered, to design brand-new suits, is a fundamental attribute of his role? Bring on, then, the stains and the tatters, and certainly no servant will take the trouble to clean the stains or mend the rips and tears. And for that matter, those suits, so quickly ravaged, will provide the providential and necessary means for another function of the nobility: paternalistic charity.

When they are blotted and moth-eaten, they can be given to the poor; and the poor, why on earth would they, in their turn, bother to patch them or remove the stains? Poor people are poor. Those rips, those stains are made to suit them, they perfectly match their social status, they elicit ever greater pity, rendered even more pleasant to the hearts of their benefactors by a sense of respect for rules and form. And so, the clothes moth is a sacred animal, even more than the she-wolf and the eagle.

The third class of society – he went on – which arrived in more recent times, does not dream of going against this ancient and time-honoured state of affairs, because this class is, yes, a sort of bourgeoisie, but a bourgeoisie in its more modern phase of expansion, so to speak, an imperialistic, clerical, and colonial expansion tantamount to armed theft. All that this class can offer is a more up-to-date and American form of the age-old customs of the other classes. For this class, too, objects have no value: what counts is merely the speed with which they can be consumed. And if, with this view in mind, the Americans have invented electric washing machines and steam irons, and other appliances ideally suited to transform, in a short time, linen and other garments into exceedingly clean but tattered rags, they are simply adapting to the same purpose more traditional weapons, predating the atomic age. It would be sufficient to allow nature, dust, insects, and moths to take their course.

(As he continued to speak, my mind followed a natural set of associations from his considerations on home economics, and I thought about how the housekeeper who for so many years had seen to the care and cleaning of my house and myself possessed, herself, innately, these same principles. I missed her, because she was a genuine character, who belonged to a genuine civilization. But she too certainly had in her veins the same scorn, at once aristocratic and plebeian, for objects and their duration. I will never taste again such delicious dishes, perfect in their simplicity, foods that seemed to have been made with such loving and painstaking care precisely because they were destined to be devoured immediately. Too soon, the veins in her legs became varicose, springing leaks like the gutters and water mains of the city of Rome, which no one ever bothers to repair. And so she left me. The woman who replaced her found, naturally enough, a vast number of rips and stains in my clothing, hung in the armoires and, since she comes from northern Italy and from the petty bourgeoisie of the nineteenth century, all the holes were patched and the house now reeks of camphor and mothballs.

Everything seems to be in order, it seems as if everything will last for a much longer time, but what sort of time? A monotonous, stingy, unimaginative, and unprotesting time, a time that refuses to accept the continuous death of things and never tosses parents from a roof, never ferociously sacrifices old age to youth. A time without derivations, without symbols, without magic, without ritual sacrifices, with neither disdain nor prodigality nor courage, excessively attached to objects, out of a fear of the slow yet inexorable death of things, a time that marches toward death. And what sort of death? Not the non-existent, theatrical death found in the most typical Roman pessimism, which culminates in the inferno,[1] which is still a form of updated exorcism. But death made up of the actual consumption, decay, and demise of those things that are so optimistically and economically identified with life that, when they finally crumble into dust, leave nothing to take their place but nothingness itself.)

My friend continued to delve into his thoughts and observations. Why – he said – while we throw away all sorts of things, as if out of a lust for throwing things away, do we never toss out, or if we do, only with the greatest difficulty, the things that really should be thrown away? Perhaps this symbol of renewal, this desire to rid oneself of death, of the remains of history, is nothing other than a ritual liberation that replaces objects entirely; and saves them all, even the dead and useless and immobile and anachronistic and irritating things? And forces us to go on living with them?

By now, it was almost dawn and, at a street corner, we said goodnight.

CHAPTER XXVI

Japanese Toys

As time goes by, festivals, the great collective feast days (the assortment of festivals that are concentrated at the junction of December and January) necessarily appear, to those who are getting on in years, increasingly obligatory, ritualistic, and conformist. They become less agreeable and more bereft to the point of vanishing entirely, with that atmosphere of expectation and hope, that pleasure of shared activity and the special occasion, that lovely imagining of meetings and discoveries, which finally linger on only as a painful recollection of one's lost youth.[1] And certainly the conformism of the holiday celebrations is something quite real to those who have experienced or observed those holiday celebrations in other times. Because the festivals and holidays, with minor modifications in style, recur, identical, in their ritual character and are new only to the new young people who, new year after new year, on the paving stones of the Piazza Navona, take the place of the old people who withdraw into their homes, locking their doors behind them.

The *Befana*, or Epiphany, in the Piazza Navona, the biggest holiday celebration of the year, the most Roman, the most ancient, with its rustic and pagan uproar, the whistles shrieking like thousands of crickets in the summer night of the chilly winter, and the raucous din of the wooden rattles, and the rural cry of sitting hens in the barnyard, and all of the baby chicks of Rome staring up at the balloons and lights, is a true mirror of the eternally unchanging. New recruits take the place of old veterans. But everything is reprised, identical, year after year, with the same stalls, stockings, and shooting galleries, in the same places, in the great, timeless cavity of the seashell-shaped piazza, with the same flowing water of the baroque fountains, and the same crowd revolving slowly around the motionless pivot of the obelisk. So that it is natural for old people to think of the day when they are dead and buried, long since serving to nourish the worms of the earth and to know that, even then, this day of celebration will not be altered in the slightest by their absence.

Each year, the variations are minimal and negligible. All that changes, and this change is grudging and slow, is the style and the quality of toys. The changes are difficult to predict. This year, for instance, you would have expected to find nothing but Sputniks, rockets, objects both lunar and stellar: but there was not a single one. Long gone are the simple toys of yore, toys that had remained the same for centuries: hoops, skipping ropes, skittles, and so on, toys that were the same for fathers and sons, that turned mothers back into little girls; traditional dolls and rocking horses were clearly in retreat, and there were only modest numbers of even such perennial favourites as helmets and breastplates, costumes of wild Indians and the Wild West, all of the stalls of the Piazza Navona this year marked the triumph, the invasion, the absolute monopoly of Japanese toys.

I don't know if children like these toys. I would tend to think not because, once the initial fascination wears off, they repeat their little show without variation and they offer children not the slightest independence or initiative of play.

They come in all kinds, there are hundreds of different types: all of them, animals, people, or objects in motion, are driven by springs with wind-up keys, or, more often, by electric switches. I don't know if children like these toys. I would tend to think not because, once the initial fascination wears off, they repeat their little show without variation and they offer children not the slightest independence or initiative of play. More than toys, they are spectacles, theatrical images. In their way, they are perfect; they are perfect in their construction, their movement, their style. They are well made, cheap, absolutely devoid of any element of folklore, any flavour, whether exotic or local, and they epitomize all the elements of modern technology, culture, and art, imitated and interpreted with painstaking and infallible attention to detail. But each one of them is (and in so refined and intelligent a way that it is almost impossible to see) a satire, or, if you like, a tiny vendetta. Their point of departure is America, and then England, and in general, the West; and Western fables of animals, both in their classical form and in the modern and Disneyesque version, abbreviated and symbolic; and Western characters, customs, and everyday life in their most distinctive incarnations.

In the animals, the satire (which becomes a satire of a satire when they refer to characters from cartoons) primarily takes the form of an astonishing increase in their mechanical perfection, with a reduction of these objects to machine-like qualities, to the point of absurdity. The dog sees a red worm on the ground, it barks, it points, it crouches, lowers its snout to the floor, leaps backwards, ventures forwards, and endlessly repeats, driven by an electric impulse, this series of psychologically perfect movements, like a machine imitating absolute spontaneity. The same thing happens with the people. Here too the satire of a mechanized and alienated world is obtained by simulating the liberty and complexity of the actions, but there is an additional element of the stereotypical, a subjective judgement, an irony that never veers over into vulgarity, but which makes these characters desperately comical. Here is the Western man about town: he is driving a sports car. He is definitely English, blond, with a moustache, and he is definitely drunk, you can see that from the way he frantically tries to brake, operating the handbrake with his left arm, while he steers crazily with his right arm on the wheel. The whole time he sits erectly in an impeccable suit, while in the transparent tubes of the racing engine, little balls chase one another, as if in a tiny illuminated game of billiards: a perfect image of total irresponsibility.

The same personality traits, irresponsible, idle, and grotesque, are found in many of these characters: housewives, perhaps Dutch housewives, preparing a meal with comic attention to detail; old sailors, possibly English, smoking a pipe; disciplinarian mothers who, turning modestly aside, spank their children's bottoms rhythmically, and so on and so forth. And here we have a magician: he sits, solemn as any character out of Dickens, at a little table upon which sits a top hat, he lifts the top hat and a white rabbit appears. He covers the rabbit with the hat again, then lifts the hat once more: the rabbit has vanished. The little game is repeated ad infinitum, with a rabbit that is there and then is gone. But the top hat, lifted and set down again and again to reveal the ambiguous truth or falsehood of the charlatan, is the traditional stovepipe hat worn by Uncle Sam, with a star-spangled hatband and a striped crown.

These toys hardly seem accidental to me. Rather, I would be tempted to think that they amount to an educational programme, putting the more advanced Western technology at the service of a subtle disdain. This is a mild, ironic, winking, innocent vendetta for the bomb on Hiroshima.

And so this Japanese invasion brings a sign of the times into the unchanging celebration of the Piazza Navona. Amidst the pagan whistles and the aroma of the eternal *torrone* ('nougat') and candyfloss, in the identically diverse crowd, in the punctual reiteration of the festive ritual, the charlatan executes, according to an electrical impulse that simulates liberty, with the impassive haughtiness of a preacher, his automaton's game.

CHAPTER XXVII

Football and Men of Letters

The flu envelops the city of Rome like a faint mist of warm droplets of sweat: a very mild flu, practically non-existent, a slight fever that disappears if you try to measure it, a weariness that is hard to say whether it comes from without or within, from the uncertain, changing weather, from exhaustion, or from a tiny epidemic. A sort of boredom, or a disgust that may come from the soul or from the latest fashions in literature or from brand-new viruses that spread, everywhere, invisibly. In this state of listless ambiguity, while you are unsure whether you should consider yourself healthy or sick, whether you ought to stay in bed or get up and go out, and every gesture and act seems burdensome, every aroma and flavour revolting, every wish incomprehensible and your body's internal sense makes the world outside a sort of moist and muggy ball of cotton wool, in which the most impelling interests are entrusted to a patience resigned to wait till tomorrow, still the phone rings, even more annoying than usual, bringing, like further burdens of illness, the demands of others, their reminders, requests, and affection.

In the absence of will and initiative, which is the chief symptom of this minimal disease, that impersonal ringing sound is, at first, practically intolerable. But then it helps to pass the hours and, however unwillingly, you find yourself feeling, for once, almost grateful to the phone, as if for a welcome but useless assistance which carries you, with its noisy and unsought imperiousness, through to the end of the day and the waning of that ephemeral fever. And then, with my spirits lifted, at least in part, I find myself picking up the phone, unlike myself, willingly, to talk to friends and, of course, I assume that they are equally willing and (even without the lassitude of the flu) happy to hear from me.

What are the dominant passions of man? Of course, it is well known that they are all based, according to theory and experience, on love; the love of things, the love of others, or of oneself; arranged by varying degree and order, right up to the most elevated passion of them all, *amor dei intellectualis*. And without doubt, the love of oneself in the context of one's work is an especially profound and justifiable passion, in the face of which it is unlikely that any other interest will win out or prevail. Now, I had spent the day not only feeling ill and fielding phone calls, but also reading the last chapters of a fine book, just published, and written by a friend.[1] When ten o'clock rolled around that evening and I had reached the last page, my mind was teeming with images, considerations, ideas of all sorts generated by my reading, complex emotions that sprang both from the literary form and from the specific content of the book, from the nature of the situation in which the characters found themselves and the ambiguous pathos of their lives and their time. And so, driven by a wish to understand these thoughts and feelings, and talk them over with the author himself, as well as to congratulate him on his creation, I dialled his number.

What are the dominant passions of man? Of course, it is well known that they are all based, according to theory and experience, on love; the love of things, the love of others, or of oneself

My friend the author, Giorgio Bassani to be specific, came to the phone, listened to my congratulations and praise, but, contrary to what I had quite reasonably expected, I heard in his voice a clear signal of haste and impatience, not customary with him and all the more surprising in that even the most modest of men will dally to receive praise, as if lured by a sweet sound. What passion, then, I wondered, could be so strong that it made my friend so brusque, so anxious to be done with a conversation that might reasonably be thought to attract his interest and delight? Understanding came to me immediately after we said our hurried goodbyes, when my eye lit on the day's newspaper. I saw that at that very hour the Spanish football team Real Madrid was playing the Italian team Juventus, and the match was being broadcast from Madrid. Clearly my writer friend had been torn away from his joyful and riveting contemplation of that spectacle by my inopportune phone call.

It seems to me that this little tale offers a particularly apt demonstration of the power of the mass spectacle, the participation in a collective adventure to which we are anonymous witnesses and yet, in relatively indirect and transposed form, physically present. That the dwarf might prefer his games to the beauty of the queen

> (nor, lest he lose a doit, his paltry stake,
> Will that discourteous churl his game forsake)[2]

is possible to understand: in the final analysis, they were two different games and the one that he chose may have been more spontaneous and voluntary to him. But that so disinterested and abstract a passion as that of viewing a distant match could win out in the heart of a man of letters or a poet, over the love of self and the paternal passion for one's own work, seems almost incredible. And yet, perhaps, each of us might have felt in some way the same sense of haste that our writer friend experienced. Some thinkers might draw lengthy conclusions on the aspects of mass civilization, on the character of alienation. We shall limit ourselves, instead, to offering this as a rare and exemplary account of how this civilization can offer such almost incredible results of humility and modesty.

CHAPTER XXVIII

The Drainage Ditch and the Measles

Until not so many years ago, Rome was still a city enclosed in a pastoral wilderness, made up of solitary countryside, expanses of burnt fields, rolling yellowish hills, swamps, and forests. The city came to an abrupt end and there began an ancient countryside, populated only by flocks of sheep: a natural nature, full of enchantment, silences, and pitfalls. This nature has now been driven so far away that only with great difficulty can you reach it or find it, and only in fragments and tatters of its former self.

Just ten years ago, during the seasonal transhumance, shepherds drove flocks of sheep through the centre of Rome, as they moved down from the high mountain pastures to the lowland plains where they would winter their flocks. I remember watching them move by night through the Piazza del Pantheon, I remember hearing them from a distance as they passed in the shadows, like a muted murmur. And even then in the meadows of the Villa Doria Pamphili shepherds would spend the winter in their huts of straw and leafy branches. Nowadays, the much more numerous flocks of cars have occupied all the streets, making it impossible for animals to pass. There is still a last large flock, behind Monte Mario, in a little hollow surrounded by blocks of flats. Sabine shepherds live there in huts like those built by Lucanians and Sardinians, and little girls go to fetch water from the surrounding houses, as they would in the country from a spring or a well. In the huts, the hearth is on the ground, in the middle of the dirt floor, without a fireplace, and hens sleep under the beds; outside, dogs keep watch over the newborn lambs. Come summer, they can no longer herd their sheep for days and days over rough paths. All the roads are filled with cars and even the flocks must be transported by lorry.

In place of that ancient nature and its ancient inhabitants and animals, there now extends all around a vast no-man's-land of temporary constructions, residences for the employees of the ministries, where an expectant population is encamped and lives. That population is waiting for everything: work, food, shelter, waiting to enter, someday, who knows when, into the city, into life. And another nature has been created, another landscape, other threats than those of the forest and malaria. For those to whom a riverbank, a piebald meadow, a well, a quarry, a dusty path, a stunted plant, and a bush are still the daily landscape of existence, the airless horizon of slavery and fantasy. And for whom every moment of life and of existence itself is uncertain, temporary, and precarious, this grey nature of the *borgate*, the grim developments on the outskirts of the city, is packed full of threats to life and limb. The weather threatens, when a sharp shower can fill the huts with water, as do the cold, the heat, the wind, rats, insects, and vermin of all sorts. Even the Roman wall, against which the hut is built, can be a threat, when an unexpected thunderstorm can cause that wall to collapse, as one did recently. The police are a threat, as likely as not to order everyone out of their imitation of a home so that bulldozers can crush it, even innocent-looking pools of water can be threats. The daily newspapers are filled with the simple tragedies that unfold here, just a stone's throw from the illustrious heart of the city, as if this were a distant forest teeming with serpents.

Yesterday I read the story, among so many others, of three children who drowned in the drainage ditch where they were playing, in a child trap of neglect and carelessness, the water drainage ditch in the middle of a field, serving the blocks of flats in the neighbourhood of San Basilio. Twelve kilometres out of town along the Via Tiburtina seems like an immense distance, separating this place from another world. What happens there, where thousands of children are banished, makes its way into the awareness of the citizenry only if it takes the form of tragedy and then it moves them to pity, for an hour, as something that happened far away, to distant folk, in the godforsaken villages of people unlike them.

Even Medea, the woman who comes to my house every morning, with a face at once grim and cheerful, to clean and cook, seems relatively unconcerned about it. She is one of them and lives in some other *borgata*, not very different in its precariousness and its unfulfilled expectations. And these stories of death are perceived as part of a hostile destiny, episodes in a long chain, which no amount of regulations or reforms are likely to alter. Today, Medea has other stories to tell me: she did not bring her little girl today, as she usually does, because, she tells me, the girl has measles. Yesterday, she left her at home for the same reason, to be looked after by another woman who lives in the same block of flats. 'You should have heard the dressing-down that her husband gave her yesterday evening! He was ready to beat her with a stick. She had gone down into the courtyard to wash clothes and my little girl followed her down. When he came back and found them both in the courtyard, he was ready to hit his wife. He didn't do it, but my goodness, how he yelled! And he said my little girl was nasty! My little girl isn't nasty. Tomorrow, if her fever drops, I'll bring her here.'

I read the story, among so many others, of three children who drowned in the drainage ditch where they were playing, in a child trap of neglect and carelessness …

Medea had no idea of what measles was, nor did she think that her neighbour, an unemployed factory worker, could have any good reason to berate his wife. She told me her story in a piercing voice, happy to be alive, brimming with joy at the yelling husband and his incomprehensible emotions, the disease, the stories that are all part of life; and her eyes glittered with an absurd, innocent happiness.

CHAPTER XXIX

A Boy Steals a Car Radio in the Piazza Navona

A little green police van was parked in the middle of the Piazza Navona, strange to behold on that paved area entirely surrounded by a single step, which preserves it, allowing children to run, words and cries to fly intact, and encompassing the enclosed and enchanted light of the sun, as if in a valley surrounded by mountains, perfect for leisurely contemplation. There it stands, parked, all day long, alongside the fountain, beside the stone horse and the stone lion that laps, tamely, at the water in front of it, watching over and protecting the restaurant 'Tre Scalini'. A bored, light-haired deputy talks, patiently, with the clamouring boys who crowd around him while, in the lonely hours of the early afternoon, Vespas zip in all directions, racing noisily, in improvised road races.

It is the only remaining sign of an event that deeply disturbed not only that venerable old neighbourhood, enclosed in a time of its own, but all of Rome. So typical and yet so extraordinary did it seem, at one and the same time: a moment of tragedy, revealing, like a sudden flash in the dark, human conditions and relations that are permanent, daily, and secret. Other gunshots, other blood, other stories and interwoven destinies may tend to obliterate the memory of that piece of urban crime, for others, like the unfailingly new waves that wash one after the other upon the beach. But not here, in Parione, where it remains an absurdity full of problems, with that Sunday in March.

In the Via dell'Anima the race came to an end, the short and furious chase that began in the piazza, when the young restaurateur, having been warned that a boy was stealing a radio from a car, someone else's car, not his, stepped out with a pistol and chased him towards the church of Sant'Agnese in Agone, beside the milk bar and the grocer's with the old sign, and past all the frightened little shops. In the Via dell'Anima (street of the *anima* 'soul': this site of relationships with the collective unconscious), in front of the printer's, he killed him with a single shot to the forehead.

This murder was immediately perceived to be an extraordinary event, both because of its absurdity and because of the distinctive identities of the two protagonists: the small-time proprietor and the member of the underclass. It undercut, as was stated at the time, the age-old homogeneity of the common folk of Rome. Common folk and writers were equally upset. The common folk expressed their collective emotions at the funeral, which was a true event, with the attendance of the entire quarter: children marching in serried ranks, with motorcycles and Vespas, the insignia of a first liberating power, women with babies in their arms, and a violent tension, an anger in which the terrifying, elemental energy of unemployed young people took shape, an energy that finds expression in gestures and expressions, since in everyday life it finds no object, no outlet. Men of culture wrote articles and essays and issued judgements. Piovene, invoking a harsh sentence for the killer, described the murder as 'horrible, reasonable to class among the most horrible crimes. It takes a monster of fear and weakness to ambush, pistol in pocket, a hapless young man who breaks an unwritten code, so providing a pretext to kill him.' Pasolini offered a perceptive psychological and historic analysis. What caught his eye was 'the existence, side by side, on the same street, in the same neighbourhood, in the centre of Italy, of two "infants", each in their own way incapable of living: the petty thief, twisted by an excess of innocence, an excess of marginalization, an excess of gratuity – all of these things likely to develop in the asocial strata of society, while the owner of the handgun, on the other hand, was twisted by a sense of entitlement, by his frivolous self-conceit, by his scorn for the poor – all things that develop in the more conformist strata of society. As always, a presocial lack of awareness and conformism tend to coincide. It is the horrifying hybrid that engendered Fascism: that is, a political phenomenon typical of less-developed nations. Twenty years ago the shooter would have been a *capo manipolo*, or Fascist squad leader, and, perhaps, the poor murdered boy, a *milite*, or militia member: an innocent militia member, aware of nothing about himself other than his own youth. Today, with the change of things, there was a murder: an atrocious, unthinkable killing… But if you think about it carefully, it is the same thing. To recruit him into the Fascist militia or to shoot him down in cold blood as a thief is the same operation of twisted middle-class conformism.'

These diagnoses are accurate. They offer an analysis of a class-driven (racist) crime: and that is precisely how the people of the quarter understood it, along with a sense of a profound insult, a criminal fracture of a natural, historic unity, and pity for themselves, the target of this insult. Then, other factors, other players in the tragedy, intervened: the dead boy's mother, the mother of his killer; and the trial began, and national publicity set to work, as if to strip them, the people of Parione, of the right to judge something that was theirs. There was a deal between the mothers, whereby, in exchange for an out-of-court settlement, the plaintiff would withdraw the charges. The judgement extended from the murder to all the other players, the other acts, the drama slowly became a novel of that Rome of the common folk, ensconced in their age-old streets, in Parione and Panico. It is a neighbourhood of artisans who enjoy a long-standing tradition (many of its craftsmen are of Spanish descent, and their ancestors came here during the reign of Pope Borgia), though most of them are now unemployed: of second-hand dealers and antiquarians, jobless people, the sort of people that society's movements and modifications tend to shove aside and yet who preserve a rare kind of virtue, a candour in basic relationships, a friendship, and a wisdom that seems to contain all the accumulated weight of an experience that comprises all of time and history: a history for which they constitute a terminus that has become immobile, and at the same time, a beginning that cannot yet fully express itself. Even the way that they speak is different from other neighbourhoods in Rome, particularly terse and, among the young, reduced practically to the simplicity of interjections, expressive of an undefined inner vitality. For these men, accustomed as they have always been to living on these same stones, there are no real class differences. Popes and mendicants are one and the same, bishops and craftsmen live in the same palazzo: what counts is the human being; everything else is consumed in the flame of time, rendered equal by death. And the dead are dead, better to worry about the living. And so the quarter closes in upon itself, in jealousy, even upon this unhappy chapter, digesting it and taking it in as yet another one of the countless events that constitute the eternal, ineluctable warp and weft of life.

Popes and mendicants are one and the same, bishops and craftsmen live in the same palazzo: what counts is the human being …

'Money can make rivers run up mountains,' says a young craftsman in the Via dell'Anima, standing in the doorway of his shop. This is his view of the settlement, the agreement between the two mothers. 'That kid who was murdered was a good kid,' he says. 'The killer, who also comes from a family that is part of the local community, a family that worked its way up from nothing, and even performed some worthy acts in the Resistance, is a "fanatic". He thought he was a sheriff. He supposedly even wore a sheriff's star. He had had a police siren installed in his car and he would chase down motorists who were committing offences, he would pull them over and fine them. In his car, he even carried a pair of regulation FBI handcuffs, as well as an American Browning, of course. He thought it was up to him to maintain order. A fanatic. He shot him in the face, you know what I mean? First he killed him, and he paid for him, because money can make rivers run up mountains.'

From the Via dell'Anima ('Street of the Soul') it's just a few steps to the Via della Pace ('Street of Peace'): a harmonious architectural enchantment. I walk under the Arco della Pace ('Arch of Peace'), past walls encrusted with time, paint, mould, thoughts, and endless succession of events. On the Piazza Montevecchio, amidst the magnificent tumbledown palazzi, a cluster of young mechanics, gleeful in their oil-stained overalls, play a game of football. The cloister behind the church of Santa Maria della Pace is silent, locked in its verdant atmosphere of moss, stones, and archways, existing prior to and long surviving any and all events, in a time all of its own, motionless and inconceivably distant.

CHAPTER XXX

The Labyrinth

This morning, when Rome first awoke, you could sense the signal of a sudden change, in the air, in the city, in things at large. The bright heat of the sun had, for the first time, a special quality, adult, mature, devoid of inner shivers, with none of the hidden chill that had lurked, like an adolescent angst, in the luminous warmth of the previous days. Summer had dropped from the sky. The greenery was still spring-like, but now it looked dense and compact, like the skin of a young woman's face that has lost the smooth transparency of adolescence. It was a natural metamorphosis, striking for its rapidity, as is always the case here in Rome, but especially pleasant for the sweet scalding sun and, as we walked around still dressed in heavy clothing, for the sense of a physical freedom to come. Boys played football on the field, the first people appeared, the vanguard of the long hours of summer, lying motionless on the grass: the change of seasons was a sign of stability.

But as we walked downhill along the street, the sounds that rose from below were different. At the bottom, when we reached the Piazzale Flaminio which, with its irregular shape and the many streets that run into it from every direction, extends outwards like a lake with many inlets, the scene that greeted the eye was one of a chaotic, unrecognizable newness. They must have worked in the still of the night, like spirits in fairytales, to build islands, flower beds, barriers, parking spaces, signals, for a new set of traffic regulations: every aspect and dimension of the place had been changed and revolutionized. On those new outlines, all across that unprecedented map of mental directives, there huddled a bleating, howling flock of confused vehicles. The new routes had been designed and carefully calculated from every single point to every other point, without crossroads, junctions, or contacts, along obligatory, circulating roads. (The idea of circulation is by now an old idea here, a sacred principle: a straight line connecting two points has been abolished in Rome. It has been discovered and it is a fairly self-evident truth that in order for traffic to circulate, it must circulate, go around in a circle. Turning and turning, in ever-widening circles and in endless spirals, the Romans thus spend hours and their entire lives.) But here, given the special complexity of the crossing traffic, arriving from all directions into the node of the piazza, it was no longer a matter of circles pure and simple. They had built, with the obstinate certainty of an abstract mind and the mechanical imagination of a robot, an inextricable geometry: a labyrinth. And in that new, rational labyrinth people were seized by a sense of bewilderment, by panic, by the most archaic of terrors.

The ancient labyrinth may have been an image of the primeval forest, and of chaos, and perhaps even of the soul inhabited by monsters: a rational reconstruction of the irrational, a place of loss and fear. The Romans, today, drove cheerfully and confidently up to their *piazzale*, or large squares, and stopped suddenly, as if they had wandered into an unfamiliar place, a dark and gloomy forest. The transformation of the place triggered in everyone (fearless motorists!) a distressing loss of existential confidence. They no longer recognized the familiar measures of their own personal world. Motionless at their steering wheels, in the tumultuous welter of roaring engines, all of them (you could see it in their eyes), while they thought they were asking traffic policemen (who did not know the answer) how to get home, were wondering where they were and who they were, unsure of themselves and disturbed by the change in the form of their world. Continuity, stability, and certainty (even in the modest appurtenances of a road surface, of a crowded, noisy street) had been abolished. In that new structure of incomprehensible limits, each of them felt rising in their chest the age-old anguish of the boundless and the shapeless, and experienced the vague vertigo of the labyrinth.

The most perfect technology, then, led to exceedingly contradictory and paradoxical consequences, since it had not been used to solve unsolved problems, nor to overcome the complexities of a chaotic world, but to give them, by crystallizing them without modifying them, an orderly appearance: to build, that is, a labyrinth. A technology that in itself was perfect, undoubtedly; but which, all the same, seemed to have forgotten one road, which happened to be the road to my house, and, if I wanted to take that road, no exit was available, apparently. In order to pass a symbolic line, along which stood a row of admonishing traffic policemen, it took me more than two kilometres of pointless, obligatory circulating, all the way out to the appalling traffic jams of Porta Pinciana. Finally, after many vain explorations, questions, and quests, I managed to discover a passage towards evening, a narrow twisting path, in the centre of that man-made welter. A road, then, existed, or had been created: but in order to find it and avoid getting lost, it was necessary (for those who come from far away) to make appropriate decisions a long time and a great distance in advance. If that decision has not been made, then you will wander into the horror without escape, the sin without salvation. Life thus becomes, necessarily, a programme, an advance decision, from the very beginning.

Upon this historical and poetic structure of imagination and free human thought that is the city of Rome, an abstract choice becomes the violent crystallization of formless chaos…

And since, in Rome, those who move about tend to follow opportunities, and want to live in the city, and not merely move from place to place, and stop to see and be seen, and shift moods and directions, the advance choice is in conflict with the nature of the city, with its very form, which is the expression of creative fantasy. Upon this historical and poetic structure of imagination and free human thought that is the city of Rome, an abstract choice becomes the violent crystallization of formless chaos: labyrinth.

Over the mechanical and anachronistic labyrinth of Rome, the impassive summer burns its precocious fires.

CHAPTER XXXI

City of Brothers

I was driving along today very slowly, meandering along really, in my car, on the boulevards of the Villa Borghese. I was taking the long way around to avoid the centre of town where traffic, turning against itself, stagnates at that time of the day, like a river in spate that carries jetsam, detritus, earth, and tree trunks, which pile up and stem the river's fury so that, running up against an obstacle that it created for itself, the stream slows, halts, swells, and overflows. In such a morass, in such a motionless labyrinth, no one can find the thread and the road down which to escape.

The sky, over the park, was luminous and grey. It seemed as if the sun was up there among the clouds like a boy lost in his adolescent thoughts: a few drops of rain left their ant tracks in the dust. The trees were cool and wet, the leaves were beginning to turn red: and the entire landscape seemed to be autumnal and spring-like at the same time, both aridly southern and mistily northern. After the downpours of the past few days, that brief interlude in which the weather appeared uncertain seemed like the end of a pointless family quarrel, when the superficial tempest is quickly forgotten because hot soup steams in bowls and everyone must sit down together at a welcoming table.

And so I was driving along, quite carefree, looking at the trees, the meadows, the birds, and the colour of the sky when, just after I rounded a corner, suddenly, without the slightest sign of trouble, the engine stopped, and there seemed to be no way to make it start again.

What could the problem be? It didn't seem like a major malfunction: there had been no odd sounds, no symptoms of real disease. I had filled the tank a little while ago: it seemed to me that the petrol, for some reason, was not reaching the engine. Or could it be some other problem? Of all the many things that, perhaps in a subconscious form of self-defence, I have chanced to forget, even though in some cases I had a really thoroughgoing knowledge, it is natural that I should have forgotten one of those things that I always least understood: the theory of engines and their operation.

The boulevard was broad and empty. A bit further on, though, I saw a cluster of young men, standing beneath the trees, who seemed to be getting ready to play football on the road with a bright blue football. I called out to them and they slowly ambled in my direction. There were five young men, all about twenty years old, tall and strong, with handsome faces and a certain shared elegance in their gestures, in the leather jacket that one was wearing or the sweater that another of them had on, or in the light-coloured raincoats tossed casually over one shoulder. I imagined that they would know much more about car maintenance than I did. As is always the case in Rome, it was impossible to say with any certainty from their appearance just who they were: whether they were poor or rich, factory workers or students or the unemployed or professionals or artisans. They immediately set to work, as if this were some new game, all of them fiddling around my car: one of them pushing it, another simply touching it, another opening the bonnet and examining the engine. I immediately understood that none of them knew a thing about cars: but they were enjoying themselves. One of them decided to get in while the others pushed, sitting where I usually did, steering my car: anyone would have thought he had never held a steering wheel in his life. And as they pushed and steered, they cracked jokes cheerfully: 'Mister, you sure have a nice car! It must be brand new! And it's an 1100, no less! The latest model! What a beautiful Jaguar! Why wait to buy a new one!' (My car is old, in fact it's very old, being a black Fiat 1100 from 1954, which has gone more than 100,000 kilometres without an overhaul. What's more, it was damaged by the explosion of a dynamite bomb in July 1960. This and other stories, and the history of the people who have ridden in the car, make it hard for me to get rid of it, though that would be the only reasonable thing to do, from every point of view.) I stood listening to those young men as they joked, the tone of their voices, at once brisk, ironic, and in some way full of fondness. Who talks that way? People only talk that way between the four walls of a room, when there is nothing separating those who speak and their relationship is one of rivalry among peers: that is, brothers, young men who are brothers, talk that way.

I stood listening to those young men as they joked, the tone of their voices, at once brisk, ironic, and in some way full of fondness. Who talks that way? People only talk that way between the four walls of a room, when there is nothing separating those who speak and their relationship is one of rivalry among peers: that is, brothers, young men who are brothers, talk that way.

I thought back to another minor episode I had observed shortly before, in the Piazzale Flaminio. A young woman, plain and wearing glasses, was driving a Fiat 500, with number plates from Bologna and in the cluttered chaos of traffic she had hit (or perhaps her car had been hit by?) a baker's van, with no serious damage to either vehicle. But traffic had come to a standstill; and the young woman, who was clearly upset, couldn't get her car to start. All around her, horns honked, impatiently and brusquely, and motorists, pedestrians, taxi drivers, and bus drivers were all yelling at her, at once brutally and jovially, 'Who gave you a driving licence?

Come on, get moving! I said, move it! Oh, so it's time for lunch? Come on, let's go!' while the young woman, bewildered, breaking into a sweat, flushing bright red, her hair unruly, her glasses fogging over, was simply unable to move: the target of a sort of group amusement that was harsh and yet, at the same time, protective.

And that is just what those young men were like, as they played around with my car. Brothers, with the slang, the language that teenage brothers use at home: full of rivalry, intimate, familiar, cruel without ill will, mischievous without hatred, brusque and violent and scornful, with a disdain that begins with themselves, with no gods or paternal hierarchies, in the pitiless condition of absolute equality.

And so it seemed to me that I understood the particular quality of Roman language and personality, that speech made up of the interjections typical of those who have known each other all their lives, who don't really need to tell each other anything. Rome is a city of brothers. It is no accident that the city's mythological roots are fraternal, based on a fight between brothers and that the father has always been, whether a god or a saint, so distant and invisible that complexities had no room to develop. Perhaps this aspect distinguishes this city from all others.

The young men had pushed my car as far as the hill and they were having fun driving it as it coasted: even rolling downhill, the engine would not start. But by this point, the car had rolled all the way down the street under its own momentum and there was a garage there. I thanked my rescuers, uncertain about how I should behave, whether I should pay them for their trouble. They did not expect payment, but they took the money I offered without surprise, without expectations of any sort, precisely the way that brothers do, happy to accept something from a brother.

At the bottom of the hill there is a field where, under the trees, about twenty young men were playing football: some wore jerseys, some wore the white overalls of shop assistants, others were dressed in uniform, children and adults, in a magnificent muddle. In the middle of the scrum, older than the rest, bald-headed and pale-faced, his dark-blue overalls stained with oil, slower than the others and thickset, my mechanic was moving the football forward with mighty kicks. He stopped playing and came over to take a look at my carburettor.

CHAPTER XXXII

Summer Dissolves in Mists

The summer dissolves in mists of heat, in vapours that wreathe suddenly upwards from the scalding roads, in the wake of the tumultuous and swollen streams that ran there, fallen from the sky and from the gutters, surging up out of the drains with yellow shades of thunderstorms. Rome is enveloped in that lukewarm watery smoke, it floats in it, wrapping itself in that lukewarm moisture as if in a bath. The sun blazes and dries up the myriad impalpable drops of water, like a giant steam iron drying the wet linen of the city's stones. Already the sky is suddenly darkening again, and stiff hard drops of astounding rain begin to fall, as if from an open tap, in a strangely mechanical way. It is the hot season of the tropical rains, as if truly, with the changes in the weather and the times, the tropics had crept all the way up here, or rather as if Rome had allowed itself, little by little, to slither downwards, just as the years, money, and standards of behaviour slither away. Plummeting down with the rain, here and there, bolts of lightning fall, crumbling to dust a few stones, a roof or two, some display windows; stopping trams in their tracks, cutting off televisions, and appearing, to the moderately terrified eyes of the citizenry, as flashes, sulphurous glows, wafting odours of ozone, warnings. In these shooting stars from other lands, in this succession of bursting splashes, flames, mists, under the sign of an aquatic and tawny lion, the hours of the day slip by until the evening arrives, with clear skies, and Rome seems to return, with the blackness of night, to its customary place, to its meridian, to its piazzas, to its *osterie*.

The Piazza Navona glitters with movement, with a lovely and wavering vitality that the shadows and mists frame in a setting of mysterious happiness, of greenery, of fountains, of giddy races, of shimmering, of gazes, of rustling velvet, of nothing.

Tables are set out on the pavement, like the benches of an open-air theatre, slowly lengthening like snakes as more diners appear on the scene, until members of large and disparate groups finally find it almost impossible to carry on conversations. The American girl who sits at the head of the table expresses her disapproval of this Roman custom of outlandishly long tables. Her blonde hair frames her odd face, with bird-like, serpentine features, in which the nose protrudes like a beak, set between her exceedingly wide-set eyes. She is Indian, one of the last Sioux women of mixed French–Canadian blood, and she is in Rome to deal in modern art. In her charming, hesitant Italian she says, 'It is an odd thing, here in Rome everything is the reverse of what we do in America. Your piazzas are round and enclosed: they seem made to spend time in and not to go anywhere; while the tables of the *osterie*, on the other hand, are narrow and long, as if people weren't meant to eat together and it is impossible to talk to one another. Where we come from, on the other hand, the streets are long and straight and they seem made to take you to the far ends of the world, while tables in restaurants are all round and everyone can hear and make themselves heard.' And so this Sioux girl was astonished at this city where no one talks to anyone but everyone lives together. Just opposite, on the other side of the fountain and its stone animals and figures, was the setting of a tragic episode, just over a year ago, in this wordless collective life. The ferocious killing of a miserable little street thief, an urchin from the alleys of Panico, murdered by a young man driven by a sadistic frenzy for law and order. This killing was viewed by the people of old Rome as especially horrifying and the café* that the killer owned and ran had long been shunned, with an almost religious fright. But now it was crowded again, filled with people attracted by the delicious ice cream and the beauty of its location, while the killer had been freed, after spending a year and three months in confinement, practically acquitted, and almost praised and held up as an example by benevolent, understanding judges. One of the diners looked over at the cafe and observed that those same judges still hold in prison, after three years, common folks of Genoa who killed no one, who hurt no one, who face no other charges than that they defended in the streets of the city civil order and liberty in the face of the Tambroni government. We all sat looking over at the cafe and a respected judge, who was sitting at our table, recalled a telegram from Tambroni himself, which had determined the direction of the magistrate's preliminary investigation in the Marturano trial, which has now reached its final phase in the court of appeal. The great judge was saying that, whether the defendants were innocent or guilty, it was judicially impossible to convict them on the basis of that preliminary investigation. He said that there was no real difference between the medieval method of the strappado and other forms of torture,

The Piazza Navona glitters with movement, with a lovely and wavering vitality that the shadows and mists frame in a setting of mysterious happiness, of greenery, of fountains, of giddy races, of shimmering, of gazes, of rustling velvet, of nothing.

* [*Translator's note.* Levi describes the same establishment as a *ristorante*, or restaurant, in the 1962 article that forms a previous chapter 'A Boy Steals a Car Radio in the Piazza Navona'. In the present chapter, based on an article written in 1963, he shifts to using the term *caffè*, or cafe. It seems likely that in the intervening year Levi had become better informed about the nature of the notorious 'Tre Scalini'.]

used to obtain evidence and proof, and the threat of six years in prison on charges of perjury, used to the same ends. He spoke of a crisis in the legal system, of the gap between that system and the conscience of the public, and about an honest judge, a close friend of ours, who had killed himself. And there were those who thought, with a sense of remorse and guilt, of the chilling reality (be it only one chance in a thousand) of an innocent person imprisoned for life without parole.

But talk is cheap, words vanish into the yielding air that fails to hold things, seeming to juxtapose them randomly, enveloping them in the opaque mists of the rainy season. Above the blurry vitality of the piazza and its happy buzzing self, events arrive from a great distance, as if borne upon a foreign wind that, as it dies, lets them fall. Truces, wars, treaties, heartfelt passions, hopes, battles, far-away earthquakes, everything is so remote: present merely as a shadow, a discussion, a tiny drop in the muggy mist. A cabinet minister at a neighbouring table says, and he of course has inside information, that the daily thunderstorms will continue for a few days, but that then the weather will change and become clear and dry, on 1 August exactly. This is an official piece of news and it cannot be questioned. Things will spring back on track, with an appropriate sense of perspective, and things will appear different, whether their scale is small or large. The tropics will drop back to their natural latitudes, and the sky will be blue and human again. In the meantime, under the sign of the Lion, Rome lies opaque in its fog of heat.

CHAPTER XXXIII

Fleeting Rome

All discourse tends quite quickly to become archaeological. All around Rome there is 'that immense and pulpy thing'[1] that is Rome, which extends outwards like an amoeba. Inside the city is a living precious world, not yet created, not fully in existence: 'a grey populace', which colours and fades from one moment to the next. At each moment it bobs to the surface, then plunges back into the depths of the objective sea of servitude; it has no language with which to express itself completely. Yet, at the same time, it is not dried out and dead like the stones and the architecture, which the sun of time tinges with a golden, ephemeral light.

Notes to the Text

by Gigliola De Donato

Introduction

1 C. Levi, *L'orologio*, Einaudi Tascabili, Turin, 1989, pp. 3–4.

2 Levi, *L'orologio*, pp. 311–12.

3 See A. Radiconcini, '"L'orologio": La Roma di Carlo Levi', in *'L'orologio' di Carlo Levi e la crisi della Repubblica*, edited by G. De Donato and P. Lacaita, Manduria, 1996, pp. 151–61 (in particular, pp. 160–1).

4 F. de Quevedo, 'A Roma sepultada en sus ruinas', from 'Parnaso español: Clio', in *Poesía varia*, edited by J. O. Crosby, Ediciones Cátedra, Madrid, 1997.

To Rome Buried in its Ruins

You seek Rome in Rome, o pilgrim!
and in Rome itself you do not find Rome:
the proud walls are a corpse
and the Aventine Hill is its own tomb.

Where the Palatine once held sway it now lies full length
and, honed by time, medals
show themselves to the battle
of the ages more as damage than as the Latin Escutcheon.

Only the Tiber remained, and its stream,
if once it irrigated Rome as a city, now weeps for it
as a sepulchre, with a grim and grieving sound.

Oh Rome, in your grandeur and beauty,
that which was solid vanishes, and all that
endures and lasts is the fleeting moment.

5 I. Calvino, *Saggi 1945–1985*, edited by M. Barenghi, Mondadori, Milan, 1995, book I, p. 1125 (the article is 'La compresenza dei tempi', which appeared in *Galleria*, xvii, 3–6, May–December 1967, pp. 237–40).

6 C. Levi, *Prima e dopo le parole: Scritti e discorsi sulla letteratura*, edited by G. De Donato and R. Galvagno, Donzelli, Rome, 2001, p. 133.

7 Levi, *Prima e dopo le parole*, p. 19.

8 See *Le mille patrie: Uomini, fatti, paesi d'Italia*, edited by G. De Donato, introduction by L. M. Lombardi Satriani, Donzelli, Rome, 2000, pp. 37–8: this is the article 'La storia è presente', published in *La nuova stampa*, 18 October 1955, featuring another charming reference to Rome: '"Here no one ever dies" is the motto of a working-class tavern on the Via Appia Antica, and it could, in a sense, be the motto and the definition of this fundamental characteristic of the history of our country. Antiquity, if it was alive, does not die in the present' (ibid.).

9 One is immediately reminded of an especially lovely scene from *L'orologio* (op. cit., pp. 140–1), with the spectacle of a 'little marionette theatre' in Piazza Margana, with an audience of 'men, women, old men, children, workmen wearing overalls, cigarette sellers, gatherers of cigarette butts, beggars, young men with glistening slicked-back hair, young women wearing short furs, toothless little old women, soldiers, office workers', triggering in the author 'an unexpected sense of joy'.

10 We should mention in any case the irony that Levi, again commenting on car traffic, but in Milan, not Rome, aims at the contemporary world, targeting in particular Umberto Eco, the neo-avant-garde, and the excessive number of 'challenges to the labyrinth' (proposed in no. 5 of *Il menabò*, which featured, among other things, Calvino's essay 'La sfida al labirinto'), in 'San Babila, Babilonia', published in *Rinascita*, 23 February 1963, now in Levi, *Prima e dopo le parole*, p. 77: 'And so listening to the *eco* ('echo'), alienating myself in my car, I

missed the street signs, Via Manzoni, Via Montenapoleone, Via San Babila, Babylon; where am I in this Milanese fog, artificial or natural, Manzoniesque, Napoleonic, Babylonian? I am in the labyrinth! Lost in the forest, too many trees, witches, fables, paths. In the labyrinth! Archetypal Minotaurean joy, metamorphosian! Quickly, I put down the accelerator, no one can see me, *mort aux vaches* ('screw the cops'), down hard, quick, quick, we challenge the labyrinth: hurry, the office is opening, hurry, free cosmic heroes of the road, we challenge the labyrinth to get there in time to clock on.'

11 See the text of Pasolini's contribution to *Saggi sulla letteratura e sull'arte*, edited by W. Siti and S. De Laude, Mondadori, Milan, 1999, book II, pp. 2647–51.

I The People of Rome

(b. 63, fasc. 1933) Two typescripts, respectively 25 and 26 pages, undated, unsigned, with a minor correction, in pen, incorporated into the second typescript. The text (in both the typescripts) features a space following the second line on p. 8, and resumes, in a new paragraph, with 'One of the 47 million ...', which is the opening line of the printed text ('Il popolo di Roma', *L'illustrazione italiana*, December 1951, special issue dedicated to Rome).

A careful word-by-word comparison of the two fragments (pp. 1–8 and 8–25/6) clearly shows, in various specific chronological references and revealing stylistic indicators, that these are two completely independent pieces of writing, merged by the author himself, or by a careless typist, or at least one who was confused by the similarity of the topics. The first fragment (pp. 1–8) dates from the years that followed July 1960: terse, concise structure, but missing parts of the version that was finally printed (see pp. 3–4); the second fragment (pp. 8–25/6) dates from no later than the publication date of December 1951.

We have restored the two texts, independently, in chronological order, under the same chapter title.

1 Carducci's poems were often taken as the target, however much they might resist, of Carlo Levi's impertinent parodies. Here, the victim is, reasonably enough, 'Nell'annuale della fondazione di Roma', *Odi barbare*, books I and III. I once happened to hear him recite from

memory, with mischievous detachment, 'Piemonte' (and he was Piedmontese!). We should also remember the amusing episode described by Antonello Gerbi ('Amico piacevole', *L'osservatorio politico letterario*, 2 February 1975, p. 67) evoking, after the death of his friend, the carefree days of their youth, when he was a guest at Levi's villa in Alassio, where they would play bowls, French tarot cards, and 'mimed poetry': 'On that occasion, we were reciting the 'Faida di comune' and Carlo, on that occasion, had the part of Tigrin della Sassetta...first he imitated to perfection, leaving us all helpless with laughter, the wicked face and spirit...and then he offered a nonchalant and dizzying send-up of the famous verse, of the medieval-style episode, of the things we learned at secondary school, and of our own adolescent pranks' (see also G. De Donato and S. D'Amaro, *Un torinese del Sud: Carlo Levi: Una biografia*, Baldini and Castoldi, Milan, 2001, p. 40).

2 See 'Il peso della realtà di Belli', in C. Levi, *Prima e dopo le parole*, edited by G. De Donato and R. Galvagno, Donzelli, Rome, 2001, p. 243.

3 This is the last line, quoted from memory, of one of Belli's best-known sonnets, 'La vita dell'omo', *Sonetti*, 774 ('death comes, and it all ends in hell').

4 This is the first of the poems in *Poesie dell'orologio*, 'Carte segrete' series, Riposati, Rome, 1950.

5 J. W. von Goethe, *Römische Elegien* (*Roman Elegies*), written during his stay in Rome from 1786 to 1788.

6 It is quite likely that Levi's reference to the aphasia of the slang of the *borgate* harks back to his preface to P. P. Pasolini's screenplay for *Accattone* (Rome, 1961), now in Levi, *Prima e dopo le parole*, p. 327.

7 See R. Scotellaro, *L'uva puttanella*, preface by C. Levi, Laterza, Bari, 1955.

8 U. Saba, 'Gratitudine, Mediterranee', 1946, in *Il canzoniere*, Einaudi, Turin, 1966.

9 Concerning Soldati's unwillingness to live with the ways of the Roman people and, in contrast, Levi's indulgence and affability in tolerating their failings, just as he appreciated their straightforward joviality, we should mention the odd exchange of articles between the two friends, in the guise of a semi-serious polemic on the subject: see, in this volume, 'City of Brothers'.

10 All of the fragment that follows, beginning with 'I saw it, too, like everyone', all the way up to and including the clause 'upon the great body of Rome', seems to have been written in a single sitting, as if in response to an upwelling of a powerful flow of simultaneous images and memories that poured forth in writing. The passage is annotated, in pen, in the author's handwriting, with a few sections in square brackets (which seem to be meant as a preliminary syntactic correction) and, in the third person, by a note in his handwriting, 'writes C. L. many years later', which seems to hint at a possible reuse of the 'piece' for another article, or as a preamble to a reprint of the first article. We mark here, with the letters A, B, C, and D, the order that the sections contained within square brackets were meant to follow.

11 Levi went there with his brother Riccardo on a special junket, which culminated in Naples, passing through Genoa, Pisa, and Florence, and happening to be in Rome precisely during the fateful days of the march on Rome, where on 4 November he was able to witness 'Mussolini kneeling at the Altar to the Fatherland. Large, but not enormous, crowd', from 'Lettere e disegni 1922–1936', *Linea d'ombra*, 55, December 1990, p. 10 (see De Donato and D'Amato, *Un torinese del Sud*, pp. 33–5).

12 This is a reference to the time he spent in prison from June to July 1935, when, as during the early period of detention, from 13 March to 19 May 1934, in the Carceri Nuove of Turin, Levi made substantial progress in his attempt to understand and identify himself and the existential crisis of his generation; from this period, there survive letters, poetry, drawings, and the relatively few pages of a 'Quaderno di prigione' ('Prison Notebook', partly published in *Galleria*, December 1967, 3–6, an issue devoted to Carlo Levi, with unpublished essays and writings and articles by many critics and men of culture, Italian and non-Italian, edited by A. Marcovecchio) of especial documentary value and of intense artistic endeavour (see, among other things, De Donato and D'Amato, *Un torinese del Sud*, pp. 96–117, with biographical and bibliographical references).

13 A concise and intense reference to the period immediately following the First World War, in Florence and Rome, which was perhaps one of the happiest periods for Levi, in terms of his political and civil experience and his artistic and literary endeavours.

14 With unassuming pride, Levi here stakes a claim to the importance of his book *L'orologio* (*The Watch*): the most complete and painstaking reconstruction, in our view, of the years between 1945 and 1948, a critical watershed in the history of our nation, for better and for worse; a great fresco of that climate of generalized fervour, burning civil tension, and conflicting passions, between the 'Vento del Nord' ('north wind') and 'return to normality'. The chief characters were the world of politics and its institutional settings, newsrooms and their editorial staff, the streets and squares in which political rallies were held; but also the little people, flowing and gathering in marketplaces, in the streets and squares of northern and southern Italy, with their remarkable inventiveness and unselfconscious vitality, in the basic struggle for everyday survival.

15 'Open City', that is to say, not garrisoned and defended in military terms, the city of Rome was recognized as such by the Vatican, as a sacred place of Christianity and a site of exceptional artistic value: but here Levi makes a bitter reference, not only to Rossellini's well-known film trilogy, but also to the fact that the city became the theatre of some of the most ferocious reprisals of the Nazis and the Fascists, as he discusses immediately below.

16 With *La noia* (*Boredom*; Bompiani, Milan, 1960), Moravia, significantly, received the Premio Viareggio, inaugurating the period of backlash and alienation, coinciding with a new school of narrative inspired by attitudes of personal introspection, a regionalism of local homelands, triggered, in a certain sense, by the case of *Il gattopardo* (*The Leopard*).

17 Aside from the text by Saba cited above (see note 8), Levi refers here to Pasolini's praise of the lumpenproletariat of Rome.

18 This is actually the last triplet of a sonnet by Quevedo, 'A Roma sepultada en sus ruinas'. (For more details, see p. xvii of the Introduction by Giulio Ferroni.)

19 See C. Levi, 'Vent'anni: I giovani', *ABC*, I, 17 July 1960. The article offers an account of the day of clashes with the police, on 6 July in Rome, following the days of clashes in Genoa and at the same time as the bloody days of clashes in Reggio Emilia and in San Ferdinando di Puglia, which followed over the course of the month in other cities of northern and southern Italy as well, in defiance of the Fascist uprising and the Tambroni government which had encouraged that uprising, availing itself of armed repression by the police and armed forces.

The demonstration in Rome had involved a procession of elderly militants, members of parliament, war widows, and former deportees and partisans, bearing wreaths to lay at the plaques commemorating the dead of Porta San Paolo, where a pitched battle had been fought with the Nazis after 25 July 1943. For Levi, the new dimension of the demonstration in 1960 resided in the fact that it was joined by an unexpected burst of popular revolt, in the form of a 'band of young people emerging from every street', to the cry of 'Resistance! Resistance!' These were the boys of Trastevere, in T-shirts, who withstood the baton blows of the police and who dodged the bullets whistling over their heads. There were those who exclaimed – according to Levi – 'They can't do anything worse than kill us!' This was the spirit of the 'New Resistance', as Levi called it (see also C. Levi, *Il bambino del 7 luglio: Dal neofascismo ai fatti di Reggio Emilia*, edited by S. Gerbi, introduction by G. De Luna, Avagliano Editore, Cava dei Tirreni, 1997).

20 As appears in a rapid sketch on the days of protest in Rome, found in a sheet of manuscript among the papers of the archive.

21 Sandro Gerbi gives an account, with a wealth of detail, of the complex and intricate events surrounding a major essay by Levi on neo-Fascism in the fifties, commissioned by his friend Max Ascoli, for the magazine *Reporter* (which Ascoli edited and published). Due to considerations of censorship, during the McCarthy era it was never published. It was not published until the nineties, in *Belfagor*, thanks to the work of the same scholar (see Levi, *Il bambino del 7 luglio*, pp. 161–203).

22 Levi's passing reference to fighting between Fascist squads and armed groups of the civilian population at the gates of Rome finds valuable confirmation in Enzo Santarelli (*Storia del fascismo*, Editori Riuniti, Rome, 1973, 3 vols [1st ed. 1967]), according to which, on the night between 28 and 29 October, Fascist squads began to converge on Rome 'amidst great difficulties', and in the zone of the Castelli Romani 'they met with sporadic armed resistance from the general populace...and, even if there was no immediate and widespread popular resistance (save for the occasional isolated battle between the Arditi del Popolo and the blackshirts in Rome, in the days that followed) this still turned a new page in Italy's national history, the history of radical and proletarian anti-Fascism' (vol. I, pp. 318 and 321). Unquestionably, this was a modest, little-known episode of resistance to Fascism on the part of the proletariat, but Levi attributed to it the emblematic value of the beginning of a new chapter in history. Quite another

matter was the fighting that involved the Roman common folk, after 8 September 1943 at Porta San Paolo, and again, later, in the same place (the location being significant) on 6 July 1960, as Levi noted immediately thereafter (see note 19).

23 See U. Saba, 'Dedica', 1944, in *Il canzoniere*, Einaudi, Turin, 1966.

II The Solitude of Rome

(b. 67, fasc. 2028) 'La solitudine di Roma', *La nuova stampa*, 8 January 1955.

III The Two-Cent Coin

(b. 67, fasc. 2028) 'La moneta da due centesimi', *La nuova stampa*, March 1955.

1 C. Baudelaire, 'Les Petites Vieilles', from the 'Tableaux parisiens', in *Les Fleurs du mal* (*I fiori del male*, translated from the French by L. De Nardis, Feltrinelli, Milan, 1973 [1st ed. 1964]).

IV Sunday Stroll

(b. 67, fasc. 2028) 'Passeggiata domenicale', *La nuova stampa*, 1 June 1955.

1 The image of the lions with what follows is reminiscent of the lines of Scotellaro, dedicated to him, which ran: 'You are better/than the four lions/that smoke, docile,/their water cigars/in the Piazza del Popolo' (R. Scottellaro, *È fatto giorno*, Mondadori, Milan, 1955; *The Sky with its Mouth Wide Open*, translated from the Italian by P. Vangelisti, Red Hill Press, Los Angeles and Berkeley, 1976).

2 G. Belli, 'Er cimitero de la morte', *Sonetti*, 583.

3 The distinctly Hemingwayesque scene that the author witnessed is clearly reminiscent of the sophisticated female protagonists and the setting of the novels *Fiesta* (or *The Sun Also Rises*) and *Over the River*

and into the Trees, as well as some of the female characters of *Forty-Nine Stories*.

4 The exhibition to which Carlo Levi refers with a certain condescension was called 'Le arti plastiche e la civiltà meccanica' ('The Plastic Arts and the Machine Civilization'), and was on display – as Pia Vivarelli informs us with interesting details – at the Galleria Nazionale d'Arte Moderna ('National Gallery of Modern Art'), from 20 May to 20 June 1955. Organized and encouraged by, among others, Leonardo Sinisgalli, it involved a number of artists, some well known for many years, such as Severini and Prampolini, and others at the height of their productivity, such as Mirko, Dova, Afro, Franchina, Consagra, Vedova, Capogrossi, and Morlotti, and, among the youngest artists, Dorazio and Perilli, standard-bearers for an entirely new visual language, who can be considered the forerunners (Novelli was still in Brazil) of the artistic neo-avant-garde.

V The Helicopter

Typescript, 6 pages, dated 6 June 1956 (b. 63, fasc. 1955), signed, title 'L'elicottero' ('The Helicopter') written in pencil by the author, with very few corrections; editorial note of acknowledgement for the cooperation of the Aeronautica Militare, or Italian Air Force, and the helicopter division of Rome's airport; published with the title 'Roma a mezz'aria' ('Rome from Mid-Air'), *Rivista Pirelli*, 4 August 1956.

1 Probably the artist Renzo Vespignani, who lived in the Piazza Jacini.

2 The 'Manica Lunga' ('Long Sleeve') is a corridor running 360 metres in length that constitutes a substantial piece of architecture adjoining the Palazzo del Quirinale, built towards the end of the sixteenth century, and subsequently enlarged – as we are told by Professor Nicola Longo – with other major structures. Among these, the 'Manica Lunga', unique for its elongated shape, is visible from the exterior for the entire length of the Via del Quirinale, which runs from the Piazza del Quirinale all the way to the Largo delle Quattro Fontane; but also from above, whence Levi's hovering eye picks it out. The construction of the 'Manica Lunga', inaugurated by Pope Sixtus V and continued by Pope Urban VIII, was completed under Alexander VI Aldobrandini (1655–67).

3 Vague echo of Leopardi's *Canto notturno*: 'Forse se avess'io l'ale/Da volar su le nubi/E noverar le stelle ad una ad una' ('Perhaps if I had wings/To fly over the clouds/And count the stars one by one').

4 Dante Alighieri, *Paradiso*, XI, lines 4–9. (Longfellow translation.)

5 This final clause echoes with implicit irony Dante's lines that follow: 'When I, from all these things emancipate,/With Beatrice above there in the heavens/With such exceeding glory was received!'

VI Apparitions in Rome

Typescript, 4 pages, undated (b. 67, fasc. 2028), with the author's signature, with the headline 'Apparizioni a Roma', *La nuova stampa*, 1 January 1957.

1 C. Baudelaire, 'Les Sept Vieillards', from the 'Tableaux parisiens', in *Les Fleurs du mal*.

VII The Duty of the Comet

Typescript, 4 pages, undated (b. 67, fasc. 2038), with the author's signature, and minor corrections; 'Il dovere della cometa', *La nuova stampa*, 5 May 1957.

1 C. Baudelaire, 'Le Voyage', from 'Fin de la mort', in *Les Fleurs du mal*.

2 G. Leopardi, *Il sabato del villaggio: Canti.*

VIII Elegy to the Mid-August Holidays

Manuscript, 8 pages, undated, unsigned, with some additions, included in the typescript, 3 pages, with the author's signature, undated, with the inclusion of various other scattered additions (b. 67, fasc. 2028); 'Elegia di Ferragosto', *La nuova stampa*, 15 August 1957.

1 This is the opening line of a quatrain in heraldic style, attributed to Francesco Lemene, since 'la bella Elpina' recurs in one of this same poet's madrigals, about whom we need offer no more extensive infor-

mation, since the reader might only consider Baretti's harsh appraisal ('La frusta letteraria', no. 10): that is, that Lemene was a 'miserable rhymester' because of his 'contrived style and poverty of thought'; and that his madrigals were 'rubbish'. Levi's passing reference to Goldoni's *Le smanie della villeggiatura* can be explained as a purely thematic allusion; less easy to explain is his use of the eighteenth-century ditty, unless this was one of those he used for one of his 'mimed poems'.

2 A species of grapevine usually cultivated on a trellis, whose white grapes ripen in July.

3 We frequently find in Levi's work the parodic use of learned citations, in this instance from Petrarch.

4 Another concealed citation, from Horace's 'hic manebimus optime'.

IX Hyperbolic Tourism

Typescript, 4 pages, undated, with the author's signature, minimal corrections of spelling (b. 67, fasc. 2028); 'Turismo iperbolico', *La nuova stampa*, 29 September 1957.

1 Dante Alighieri, *Purgatorio*, III, line 79 and following. Levi's use of literary citation – as we have said – often has a slight parodic inflection. Here the Dantesque comparison is barely hinted at, with a lordly stylistic disdain, levelled at the obtuse nature of mass culture. It is appropriate to quote the passage from Dante in its entirety (Longfellow translation): 'As sheep come issuing forth from out the fold/By ones and twos and threes, and the others stand/Timidly, holding down their eyes and nostrils,/And what the foremost does the others do,/ Huddling themselves against her, if she stop,/Simple and quiet and the wherefore know not...And all the others, who came after them,/ Not knowing why nor wherefore, did the same.' (Levi just before, with tacit anticipation, had written, paraphrasing Dante, 'to do what others do'.)

2 L. Ariosto, *Satire* (III, lines 61–3): 'This is enough for me; the rest of the world/without ever paying the innkeeper I shall go seeking/with Ptolemy, whether the world is at peace or war.'

X Killing Time

Manuscript, 5 pages, 1 January 1958, with the author's signature, with various additions and corrections, some in red ink, included in the typescript (4 pages, undated, with the author's signature), with a few additions (b. 68, fasc. 2031); 'Ammazzare il tempo', *La nuova stampa*, 7 January 1958, with a small oversight.

XI Points of View

(b. 68, fasc. 2031) 'I punti di vista', *La nuova stampa*, 5 February 1958.

XII The Power of the Poor

Draft manuscript, with corrections, interrupted on the reverse of the unnumbered page, untitled, undated, unsigned; typescript, 4 pages, undated, with the author's signature (b. 68, fasc. 2031); 'Il potere dei poveri', *La nuova stampa*, 28 March 1958.

XIII Brigands and Peasants

Typescript, 5 pages, undated, with the author's signature (b. 68, fasc. 2031); 'Briganti e contadini', *La nuova stampa*, 8 April 1958.

1 R. Scotellaro, *Contadini del Sud*, introduction by M. Rossi Doria, Laterza, Bari, 1955.

XIV Plants and Seeds

'There are things that stay in their places…' is the opening of the manuscript, abandoned on the first page as far as 'cages with birds hung', where the author wanders off into a list of various types of birds (tawny pipit, quail, goldfinch, canary), and adds, in a new paragraph: 'Names count, names carry weight. Here peace covers a perfect, humble world with its enchantment. On the far side of Rome…', which is only continued on p. 3.

Complete typescript, 4 pages, 24 April 1958, with the author's signature, with scattered additions and corrections, entitled 'La pace e il diavolo' ('Peace and the Devil'), with the author's suggested alternative title 'Piante e semi' ('Plants and Seeds'), (b. 68, fasc. 2031); *La nuova stampa*, 27 April 1958.

1 'In our time shall the righteous flourish; yea, and abundance of peace, so long as the moon endureth.'

XV The Steps of Rome

'A world are you, O Rome' is the opening line of the partial manuscript, 2 pages (undated, unsigned), which is found incorporated at p. 3 (first paragraph), with modifications and improvement of the text itself, extensively integrated, in the typescript, 5 pages, undated, signed, with the addition of the first 2 pages and the title 'Lo scalino di Roma' ('The Steps of Rome'), (b. 68, fasc. 2031); *La nuova stampa*, 25 July 1958.

1 Goethe, *Römische Elegien*.

XVI The Empty Cities

Manuscript, 2 pages, undated, unsigned, in red ink, written on 3 sides, in distinct fragments and in a rough draft, only partially corresponding with the typescript (3 pages, 18 August 1958, with the author's signature, only a few minor corrections), (b. 68, fasc. 2031); 'Le città vuote', *La nuova stampa*, 21 August 1958.

1 G. E. Haussmann (Paris, 1809–91), well-known politician and urban planner, who designed and partly built the layout, in modern terms, of the city of Paris, substantially transforming the structure of a city that was still medieval in many ways, in keeping with basic principles of expanse and representation: great emphasis given to public buildings, construction of broad boulevards, reclamation of water supply and sewer systems, extension of the urban area to the surrounding towns. Levi alludes to this sense of the monumental with reference to the Madeleine, leaving aside his reservations about surgical operations in historic centres, for the sake of a certain imperial grandeur. Here, what is implicit is the reference to the urban devastation inflicted by Fascism

upon Rome (see Levi, *Le mille patrie: Uomini, fatti, paesi d'Italia*, edited by G. De Donato, introduction by L. M. Lombardi Satriani, Donzelli, Rome, 2000).

2 E. De Martino, *Morte e pianto rituale nel mondo antico*, Boringhieri, Turin, 1958: The topic of *passione vegetale* – as Clara Gallini, well-known scholar who has studied De Martino, points out – has to do with the myths and rituals of the ancient Mediterranean region in connection with the killing of the harvest god (see the chapter 'La messe del dolore', or 'The Harvest of Grief'), and was reprinted with the modified title of *Dal lamento funebre antico al pianto di Maria*, with an extensive introductory essay by Clara Gallini. It does not appear that Levi ever got around to writing a review of the book, as none can be found in the archives, and Gallini herself is not aware of one, and she is still the director of the De Martino Collection.

XVII Girls and Trees

Manuscript, 4 pages (unnumbered), undated, unsigned, a first structured draft of the text; first typescript, 4 pages, undated, with the author's signature in block letters, numerous interpolations and substantial additions in pencil, with a title, in parentheses, of 'Ragazze e alberi' ('Girls and Trees'), and a second typescript, 4 pages, undated, signed, same title, with corrections incorporated and a first title of the author (which we confirm) in pencil in the margin (b. 68, fasc. 2033); published *La stampa*, 19 April 1959, with the editorial title of 'Primavera a Roma' ('Spring in Rome').

1 Levi's invariably acute interest in urban planning offers us here a quick account of the Turinese imprint on the Prati quarter (named after the *prati*, or 'meadows', that once extended from Castel Sant'Angelo – as Romans all know very well – to the area occupied by the quarter that takes that name). During the 1880s and 1890s – as I am informed by my friend Nicola Longo with his authoritative precision – the area was designed by Piedmontese planners in keeping with a rationalist approach to urbanization, which Turin had in turn borrowed from Paris. Hence the coordinated structure of the large 'star-shaped' piazzas (Piazza Risorgimento, Piazza Cavour, Piazza Mazzini, Piazza della Libertà, Piazza degli Eroi, and Piazza Bainsizza) with roads converging in a spoke pattern, alternating with the broad, tree-lined boulevards, or *viali* (Viale Giulio Cesare, Viale delle Milizie, Viale Angelico, Viale

Mazzini, and so on). Levi, in keeping with a style all of his own, barely hints at these aspects, while steeping them in the dreamy lightness of his gaze.

2 Levi refers to one of Brecht's characters, Herr Keuner (present in a number of different pieces of Brecht's writing), who served as the mouthpiece for his unpopular ideas. The collected text of these writings clearly included, in an edition that is no longer available, *Gli affari del Signor Giulio Cesare* (Einaudi, Turin, 1957).

XVIII A Dawn in Rome

Manuscript, 7 pages, undated, unsigned, with numerous integrations and marginal corrections in red ink, corresponding, with minimal variants, to a typescript entitled 'I galli e l'usignuolo' ('The Cocks and the Nightingale'), 3 pages, undated, signed (b. 68, fasc. 2033); published with the title 'Un'alba a Roma' ('A Dawn in Rome'), *La stampa*, 16 May 1959.

1 G. Parini, 'e a te soavemente i lumi chiuse/il gallo che li suole aprire altrui', from 'Il mattino', *Il giorno* (lines 56–7).

XIX Summer Journey

'This year, summer…' is the opening of the manuscript, 3 pages, two of which written front and back, undated, unsigned, with numerous corrections and additions in pencil and pen, included in the typescript, approximately 4 pages, with three minor corrections, undated, signed, entitled 'Viaggio d'estate' ('Summer Journey') (b. 68, fasc. 2033), *La stampa*, 13 August 1959.

1 In keeping with his customary moderation of style, set somewhere between a learned discourse and everyday speech, Levi implicitly refers (rightly so) to the origins of the literary character, from the drama written by the Spanish author Tirso da Molina (1630), to the short poem by Lord Byron, and of course to *Don Giovanni* by Mozart and Da Ponte. Levi, in fact, captures something of that tragic sense in the intense attention of the children, frightened by the scene of the final catastrophe; see also 'Sunday Stroll', in this same volume.

XX The New Moon

Typescript, 3 pages, undated, signed (b. 68, fasc. 2033), 'La luna nuova', *La stampa*, 20 September 1959.

1 A fragment that Leopardi had first entitled 'Lo spavento notturno' (composed in Recanati in 1819). The poet, in the figure of a shepherd (Alceta) tells Melisso that he had dreamed of how the moon had suddenly come loose from the sky and had hurtled to earth amidst thousands of sparks, landing in the meadow outside his house: this may have been the poet's first naive and at the same time profoundly moving contemplation of the moon: 'in such guise/that I was chilled with fear; and still I am uncertain.' Levi's citation of this poem serves to express a special distaste for the din and chatter that accompanies the extraordinary event of the 'collapse of a limit', the end of the untouchability of a myth, reduced in stature to that of an 'arid, dusty desert', 'by the rocket [that] had reached the moon'. And so the writer perceived the moon, which continued to ride in the sky, as 'a little closer, a little more pitiable'.

2 A well-known aria from Vincenzo Bellini's *Norma*, in which the female protagonist confides to the moon her sorrows of love and her presentiments of death. This – Levi seems to be suggesting – is what the moon once represented!

XXI San Lorenzo and San Paolo

First typescript, 4 pages, undated, signed (with notes that can be determined to refer to the events of July 1960, to which the title 'San Lorenzo e San Paolo' ('San Lorenzo and San Paolo') also refers, censored and modified by the newspaper's editors); second typescript, 'Un lume passa volando' ('A Fleeting Illumination'), 3 pages, signed, with the title in the margin at top right (b. 68, fasc. 2035); *La stampa*, 18 August 1960, with the modifications included. We have restored the author's original text and title.

1 We have included in the text, set within square brackets, a number of notes in the author's hand, written in pencil and scattered here and there, the last of which – 'Think of 25 August' – is an indicator of later additions to the printed text.

2 The reference is to the well-known events of July 1960. Please refer to note 19 of 'The People of Rome' (Chapter I), in this volume.

3 He refers to Pascoli's exceedingly well-known poem 'X Agosto' ('San Lorenzo, io so perché tanto/di stelle, per l'aria tranquilla/arde e cade, perché sì gran pianto/nel concavo cielo sfavilla'), towards which Levi expresses certain reservations, pointing out certain aesthetic and 'excessively sentimental' curvatures of style which, while not glaring, in this verse, certainly represent the looming risk always found in Pascoli's lyricism: a limitation – I would add – that, while it may not diminish his greatness, nevertheless affects his forms, sometimes elevating them to an expressive absoluteness of great modesty and formal clarity, at other times fragmenting them with the aura interposed by what Levi calls 'the taste of sentiment'. Also note the interesting comparison with Umberto Saba, always the poet of his heart, whom he considered more modern, indeed, entirely *novecentesco* ('of the twentieth century'). One should note, by the way, that Pascoli is described as 'this Montale of the time', which was later erased.

XXII A Child in Flight

Manuscript, 10 pages, including 4 pages written on the reverse; only the first 4 pages are numbered and they coincide, roughly, with pages 1–2 of the typescript; the other 3 pages (4 sides of the manuscript), very difficult and practically indecipherable, do not coincide with the typescript (3–4 pages); lastly, the manuscript, last 3 sides, and typescript, pages 4 (last paragraph), 5, and 6 (b. 68, fasc. 2035) coincide; 'Un bambino che vola', *La stampa*, 13 September 1960.

1 A character in Leo Tolstoy's *War and Peace*, whom Levi identifies in various critical writings as the most symbolically intense expression of happiness inasmuch as she represents a unique and unrepeatable instant of the vital emotion of youth, that is, the nascent phase of each and every individual, just as in the lives of peoples, in the act of recognizing themselves in the creative moments of history (see Levi, *Prima e dopo le parole*, pp. 155–9).

2 See Scotellaro, *L'uva puttanella*, in the pages dedicated to *Cristo si è fermato a Eboli* (*Christ Stopped at Eboli*), during Scotellaro's time in prison.

XXIII After the Party

Manuscript, 9 pages, unnumbered, in red ink, undated, unsigned, with numerous corrections and additions; typescript, 3 pages, undated, signed, with a few minor typographical errors (b. 69, fasc. 2039); 'Dopo la festa', *ABC*, section 'Parole chiare', 18 September 1960.

1 The obelisk takes its name from the ancient capital of the Coptic kingdom in Ethiopia, founded in the Christian era, which flourished in contact with Rome and Byzantium, as well as with Persia, and then vanished with the expansion of Islam. Among the archaeological remains there are many obelisks, one of which was taken to Rome and set up in the Forum, near the Arch of Constantine under the Fascist regime.

2 A well-known architect and architectural historian, he worked with great cultural and civic engagement for the preservation of the artistic and architectural heritage, denouncing the ravages of reckless speculation in real-estate development.

3 Architect and urban planner from Verona, also active in Rome, who was skilled and culturally important in the safeguarding of the artistic heritage.

XXIV Substance and Chance

Typescript, 4 pages, undated, signed (b. 69, fasc. 2039), 'Sostanza e accidente', *ABC*, section 'Parole chiare', 13 November 1960. The writer describes in many ways a moment (July 1960) of particular ideological and civil tension, rich in significance: hence the glistening, subtle irony that Levi directs towards the powerful political leader on the opposing side, diminished, in any case, not only by his very audience, dragged in from the surrounding countryside like a flock of sheep to fill the Piazza del Popolo for a rally, which it witnesses with an opaque, passive attitude; but also by the boredom and preachy aura surrounding the speech itself, rendered even more miserable by the comparison (which Levi succeeds in using as a counterpoint) with the immaterial and luminous presence of the great Stendhal, whom he evokes.

1 H. B. Stendhal, *Roma, Napoli e Firenze*, Italian edition of *Rome, Naples et Florence*, preface by C. Levi, Parenti, Rome, 1960 (1st ed.), later republished by Laterza (see Levi, *Prima e dopo le parole*, pp. 133–45 and 315).

2 Well-known film by Luchino Visconti.

XXV Clothes Moths

(b. 69, fasc. 2039) 'Le tarme', *ABC*, section 'Parole chiare', 8 January 1961.

1 Implicit quotation from Belli (see 'The People of Rome' (Chapter I), in this same volume).

XXVI Japanese Toys

(b. 69, fasc. 2037) Typescript, about 5 pages, undated, with the author's signature, a few corrections; 'I giocattoli giapponesi', *La stampa*, 11 January 1962.

1 Note the Leopardian flavour, which takes once again an understated tone: 'of that vague imagining...of the long-lost youthful age.'

XXVII Football and Men of Letters

Typescript, 3 pages, undated, with the author's signature, minimal corrections (b. 69, fasc. 2037); 'Calcio e letterati', *La stampa*, 27 February 1962.

1 He is referring to *Il giardino dei Finzi Contini* (Einaudi, Turin, 1962), for which Giorgio Bassani won the Premio Viareggio that year.

2 L. Ariosto, *Orlando furioso*, XXVIII, canto 38.

XXVIII The Drainage Ditch and the Measles

Typescript, 3 pages, undated, signed, just a few corrections, entitled 'La marrana e il morbillo' ('The Drainage Ditch and the Measles') (b. 69, fasc. 2037), published with the title 'Vita delle "borgate"' ('Life in the "Borgate"'), and a subtitle of 'Dai pastori ai sottoproletari di Roma' ('From the Shepherds to the Lumpenproletariat of Rome'), *La stampa*, 17 April 1962.

XXIX A Boy Steals a Car Radio in the Piazza Navona

Typescript, 5 pages, undated, with the author's signature; identified in the archives with various titles, such as 'Ciampini' and 'Un ragazzo che rubava autoradio a Piazza Navona' ('A Boy Steals a Car Radio in the Piazza Navona'); dated, according to reliable evidence, between April and May 1962 (b. 71, fasc. 2083). Based on a well-known killing that shocked public opinion at the time, the article, for reasons that were not spelled out but which can be easily guessed at, was not published by *La stampa*, although Levi had a regular contribution agreement with the paper, as is well known.

XXX The Labyrinth

Typescript, about 4 pages, undated, with the author's signature, entitled 'Il labirinto' ('The Labyrinth') (b. 69, fasc. 2037); *La stampa*, 1 May 1962, with the title 'Sorpresa a Roma' ('Surprise in Rome').

XXXI City of Brothers

Typescript, 4 pages, undated, signed (b. 69, fasc. 2037); 'La città dei fratelli', *La stampa*, 25 November 1962, with the subtitle 'Il vero spirito di Roma' ('The True Spirit of Rome'). The article prompted a semi-serious polemic with Levi's friend Mario Soldati (who was writing for *Il giorno*), while Levi replied in *La stampa* (6 December 1962).

XXXII Summer Dissolves in Mists

Typescript, 4 pages, datable to August 1963 (b. 69, fasc. 2037), not published due to 'cessation of his contract with *La stampa*, due to Carlo Levi's candidacy for the Italian senate as an independent affiliated with the Italian Communist Party', as we read in the notation of the archive; unpublished.

XXXIII Fleeting Rome

Manuscript, one page, dated 6 March 1963, unsigned (b. 70, fasc. 2061); unpublished fragment.

1 A distinctly Pasoliniesque epithet (see, for instance, *Una vita violenta*, or *A Violent Life*) a clear indicator of the fact that Levi borrowed from his technique and style.

Basic Chronology of Carlo Levi's Life

by Sergio D'Amaro

1902	*29 November* At 12.45 a.m., Carlo Levi is born. He is the son of Ercole Levi and Annetta Treves; his mother is in turn the sister of the Socialist leader Claudio Treves and of Marco Treves, a psychiatrist. Upon learning of the birth, C. Treves sends the family a picture postcard of Mazzini.
1915	He paints his first canvas, depicting a dawn and his own home.
***c.*1917**	He executes his first portrait, inspired by Dürer's *Self-Portrait with Glove* (see the catalogue *Carlo Levi si ferma a Firenze*, edited by C. L. Ragghianti, Fratelli Alinari, Florence, 1977, p. 28).
1917	After attending secondary school at the Liceo Alfieri, he enrols in the Department of Medicine at the University of Turin.
1918	*November* He meets Piero Gobetti. *Energie nove* begins publication.
1921	Occupation of the Società di Cultura by Gobetti's group. Levi also takes part, and speaks jokingly of a 'coup d'état'.
1922	*October/November* While travelling with his brother Riccardo, he visits Florence, Rome, and Naples. He begins working for Gobetti's weekly magazine *La rivoluzione liberale*.
1923	He exhibits a portrait of his father at the Quadriennale in Turin. Gobetti's publishing house is founded. He meets Casorati through Gobetti.

1924 He gains a first-class degree in Medicine. He exhibits at the XIV Venice Biennale. The group at *La rivoluzione liberale* votes for the Communists during the general election. He has been romantically involved with Maria Marchesini for some time. At the home of Giacomo Debenedetti he meets Umberto Saba, whom he will see again in Florence during the Nazi occupation.

1924–8 He works with Professor Micheli at the medical clinic of the University of Turin. He does experimental work on liver disease and diseases of the bile ducts. In Paris, he attends postgraduate courses with Professors Bourguignon, Vidal, Besançon, and others.

1925–6 He does his national service, first in Florence and then at the Moncenisio. He mixes with the Rosselli brothers. He witnesses the attack on Salvemini.

1925 First stay in Paris. He has a studio in la rue de la Convention.

1 November The weekly *La rivoluzione liberale* is obliged to cease publication. He meets Edoardo Persico, who moved to Turin that year.

1926 *16 February* Gobetti dies.

His family purchases the villa in Alassio. He publishes an article, 'Soffici a Venezia', in *Il Baretti*. He takes part in the XV Venice Biennale.

1927 Second stay in Paris. He develops a romantic attachment to Vitia Gourevitch. He meets M. Andreis and A. Garosci. He takes part in the *Baretti* meetings in the Via Fabro, and talks with Monti, De Rosa, Passerin d'Entrèves, and Brosio. He decides to devote himself entirely to painting.

1928 Third stay in Paris. *Il Baretti* ceases publication.

1929 With Nello Rosselli and Riccardo Bauer he founds *La lotta politica*. He takes part in the exhibition 'Sei pittori di Torino', with J. Boswell, G. Chessa, N. Galante, F. Menzio, and E. Paulucci. The exhibition travels to Turin (January), Genoa (April–May), and Milan (November).

In August the Giustizia e Libertà ('Justice and Liberty') movement is founded. The Rosselli brothers escape from the islands of Lipari.

Levi moves his Paris studio to la rue du Cotentin.

1929–31 With M. Andreis he is in charge of the organization of the Turin group Giustizia e Libertà. He designs stamps and the cover of Lussu's book *La catena* with the symbol of Giustizia e Libertà.

1930 He takes part in the XVII Venice Biennale. Second Turinese exhibition of the 'Sei pittori' at the Sala Guglielmi in Turin.

With Menzio and Paulucci, he exhibits at the Bloomsbury Gallery in London, with a catalogue introduction by Lionello Venturi.

25 November to 5 December Group exhibition of the Novecento Italiano in Buenos Aires.

He paints *L'eroe cinese* (*The Chinese Hero*).

1931 *January* He exhibits at the Galleria d'Arte di Roma.

He contributes to the Turin newsletter *Voci d'officina*, edited by R. Poli, M. Andreis, A. Garosci, L. Scala, B. Allason, A. Rho, and others. He takes part in the composition of the *Programma rivoluzionario di 'Giustizia e Libertà'*, with Carlo Rosselli, Lussu, Tarchiani, Salvemini, and Nitti. Many of the members of Giustizia e Libertà also contribute to Einaudi's *La cultura*.

In Rome, along with Paulucci, he begins to work on film sets for the 'Cines' studio. He works on the films *Patatrac* (G. Righelli) and *Ricordo d'infanzia* (M. Soldati).

He comes into contact with Guttuso.

December He exhibits with Chessa, Menzio, Paulucci, and Spazzapan at the Parisian gallery 'Jeune Europe', with a catalogue introduction by L. Venturi.

1931–2 In Paris, he meets Stravinsky and Prokofiev. He is in close contact with Garosci, Ferrata, and L. Ferrero, regularly meeting them at the 'Rouget' restaurant on le boulevard Saint-Michel.

Meetings with Noventa, Moravia, and Chiaromonte. He spends time with De Chirico, Severini, and Tozzi.

1932 *June* First solo exhibition in Paris at the 'Jeune Europe' gallery.

He takes part in the XVIII Venice Biennale. He publishes, in the *Quaderni di Giustizia e Libertà*, his 'Seconda lettera dall'Italia' ('Second Letter from Italy') and 'Il concetto di autonomia nel programma di Giustizia e Libertà' ('The Concept of Autonomy in the Programme of Justice and Liberty').

1932–3 He serves as an intermediary between Turin and the refugees.

1932–4 He spends nearly all this time in Paris.

1933 He attends the Paris funeral of his uncle Claudio Treves.

He publishes in the *Quaderni di Giustizia e Libertà* 'In morte di Claudio Treves e Piero Gobetti e la rivoluzione liberale' ('On the Deaths of Claudio Treves and Piero Gobetti and the Liberal Revolution').

March He moves to no. 6 Villa Chauvelot, Paris XV.

June Solo exhibition at the 'Bonjean' gallery.

He is in touch with Unafilm.

1933–5 He works in the organizational centre of Giustizia e Libertà, with Vittorio Foa and Leone Ginzburg.

1934 *13 March* He is arrested at Alassio and interned in Turin prison for suspected participation in the movement of Giustizia e Libertà, in the wake of the arrest of S. Segre and the escape of Mario Levi to Ponte Tresa ('the Togo affair').

26 April The magazine *La libertà* publishes an appeal by a number of artists living in Paris (including Léger, Chagall, Derain) for Levi's release.

9 May He is released. The Commissione Provinciale per l'Ammonizione e il Confino di Polizia ('Provincial Commission for Warning and Police Internment') orders special warning status for two years. His request for the drawings he did in prison is rejected.

He works with Soldati at Lux Film, under the supervision of the musicologist Gatti.

He takes part in a travelling exhibition in the United States.

1934–5 Long stays in Alassio, alternating with time in Turin.

He continues his relations with Foa and *La cultura* (Einaudi, Antonicelli, Pavese, Cajumi, etc.), where he signs his work with the pseudonym 'Tre Stelle' ('Three Stars').

1935 *April* He designs the cover for M. Soldati's book *America primo amore*.

15 May He is arrested in Turin.

23 May He is questioned by the political police in Turin and subsequently transferred to the prison of Regina Coeli in Rome.

15 July The Commissione Provinciale di Roma per l'Assegnazione al Confino di Polizia ('Provincial Commission of Rome for Assignment to Police Internment') condemns Carlo Levi to three years' internment, to be served in Grassano (Matera province).

23 July He submits an appeal to the Commissione di Appello ('Appeals Commission').

3 August He arrives in Grassano. First he stays at the hotel run by L. Prisco, then in a house owned by the Schiavone family. During his period of internment he paints at least 70 canvases.

20 August Paola Levi arrives (he is now romantically involved with her, and she will bear him a daughter in 1937), and leaves again on 2 September.

30 August The prefect of Matera suggests to the minister of the interior that Levi be transferred to Aliano, to prevent him from receiving luggage and friends that might elude censorship.

17 September His sister Luisa arrives in Grassano.

18 September He is moved to Aliano. He takes a room at the Albergo Moderno.

23 September He draws up a list of the people with whom he intends to correspond.

5 October His sister Luisa leaves for Turin.

20 October He stays in a house owned by relatives of the arch-priest of Aliano.

30 November He is in Grassano for a week, to finish a few paintings.

1935–6 He develops a plan for drainage and reclamation, and for prevention of malaria, in the Aliano area.

1936 *9 February* Letter of protest to the *questore*, or chief of police, of Matera concerning the prohibition against him practising medicine.

February–March He is in Turin following the death of an uncle.

1 May Inauguration of the exhibition of the Società Promotrice di Belle Arti di Torino ('Turin Society for the Encouragement of Fine Arts'). Levi takes part, with three canvases of Lucanian subjects.

20 May The minister of the interior orders the liberation of all political internees, in commemoration of the proclamation of the Italian Empire.

26 May Levi leaves for Turin, where he resumes his political activity.

November Solo exhibition at the 'Il Milione' gallery in Milan, in which he exhibits paintings he did while in political internment.

December Solo exhibition at the 'Genova' gallery in Genoa, with a catalogue introduction by G. Ferrata.

1937 *May* Solo exhibition at the 'La Cometa' gallery in Rome, with a catalogue introduction by S. Solmi.

10 June Assassination of the Rosselli brothers at Bagnoles-sur-l'Orne. Levi paints an *Autoritratto con la camicia insanguinata* (*Self-Portrait with Bloody Shirt*).

November Set designer in Rome for the film *Pietro Micca*.

December He exhibits in New York in the 'Anthology of Contemporary Italian Painting'.

1938 He composes, in Nice and Cannes, a number of short verses in intimist and elegiacal style. Long winter evenings spent in the company of F. Venturi, A. Garosci, and P. Vittorelli. He contributes to the weekly *Giustizia e Libertà*.

1939 Obliged to escape to France, he is at La Baule, near Saint-Nazaire in Brittany, from September to December. Here he writes, while reading Vico and the Bible, *Paura della libertà* (*Of Fear and Freedom*).

1940 He spends time in Cannes and Marseilles. During this period, he refuses to go to the United States, although he could easily have taken advantage of the international visa extended by Roosevelt to all persecuted European intellectuals.

1941 He returns to Italy. In Milan, he meets Ugo La Malfa in order to agree on the terms and means by which the clandestine struggle will be carried on.

1942 He joins the Partito d'Azione ('Action Party').

He writes the essay 'Paura della pittura' ('Fear of Painting', later published, in 1948, in Carlo Ludovico Ragghianti's monograph on Levi). He moves to Florence, where he becomes one of the leading figures in the Partito d'Azione. He has a studio in the Piazza Donatello. He meets or spends time with Delfini, Montale, Gadda, Bazlen, Q. Martini, Cancogni, Tobino, Antonicelli, Timpanaro Sr, and P. Santi.

1943 *April* He is arrested and taken to prison, or the Carcere delle Murate, where he remains until 26 July.

September He is a guest of Montale when 'the days of misfortune' begin. Montale himself was to welcome many anti-Fascist partisans and members of the Comitato di Liberazione Nazionale (CLN).

December 1943 to July 1944 In Fiesole, and later in Florence in the Piazza Pitti, where he continues to live in hiding, he writes *Cristo si è fermato a Eboli* (*Christ Stopped at Eboli*). In this period, he meets Saba once again, and also meets his daughter Linuccia, who will become his partner until his death.

1943–4 He executes a number of monotypes on the theme of the war, either as lived or as foreshadowed.

1944 Following the liberation of Florence (11 August), he acts as a representative of the Partito d'Azione to the Comitato Toscano di Liberazione Nazionale.

September He becomes deputy director of the daily *La nazione del popolo*, mouthpiece of the CLN.

1943–5 He serves as a member of the press commission of the CLN and on the commission of architects and technicians for the reconstruction of the historical centre of Florence.

1945 *24 April* He is named chairman of the commission on urban planning and construction for the committee for the reconstruction of the province of Florence.

June He moves to Rome, where he works as the director of *L'Italia libera*, national publication of the Partito d'Azione, until February 1946.

Einaudi publishes *Cristo si è fermato a Eboli*. The book is translated into various languages and becomes a best-seller in the United States.

1946 The founding manifesto of the Nuova Secessione Artistica Italiana is published: among the signatories are Levi, Birolli, Cassinari, Guttuso, Leoncillo, Morlotti, Pizzinato, Santomaso, Vedova, and Viani.

April Solo exhibition at the Galleria del Bosco in Turin.

May He runs as a candidate for the Costituente ('Constituent Assembly'), affiliated with the Alleanza Repubblicana ('Republican Alliance') party, along with Dorso, Fiore, and Rossi-Doria, in the ward of Bari-Foggia and that of Potenza-Matera, where he returns for the first time since his internment. In Basilicata (Lucania), he meets Rocco Scotellaro. He receives 252 votes.

December Solo exhibition at the 'Lo Zodiaco' gallery in Rome, with a catalogue introduction by Ragghianti.

He begins contributing to *La stampa*. He publishes *Paura della libertà* (*Of Fear and Freedom*).

1947 *May* First American solo exhibition at the Wildenstein Gallery in New York.

December He is present at the founding conference of the Fronte del Mezzogiorno.

He is a participant in the Movimento per la Pace ('Movement for Peace'): he meets, among others, Neruda and Curie.

1947–8 He does a series of satirical cartoons for the daily *L'Italia socialista*, directed by Garosci.

1948 He exhibits at the XXIV Venice Biennale, in a hall of his own. The Fronte Nuovo delle Arti enjoyed great success in Venice.

February Solo exhibition at the 'L'Obelisco' gallery in Rome.

Edizioni U in Florence publishes Ragghianti's monograph on his oeuvre as a painter.

1949 He takes part in the Assise del Mezzogiorno with Amendola, Gatto, and Quasimodo.

1950 He takes part in the Congresso della Resistenza ('Congress of the Resistance') in Venice. He publishes *L'orologio* (*The Watch*) with Einaudi.

1951 *January* He takes part in the second art exhibition against barbarity at the Galleria in Rome, organized by the realist painters Penelope, Guttuso, Mafai, Trombadori, and Socrate, in response to Eisenhower's visit.

He writes a series of articles on the flooding of the Polesine.

1951–2 He travels through Calabria, from Melissa to the Sila, accompanied by Scotellaro. He also visits Sicily and Sardinia.

1952 *March* Solo exhibition at the 'La Colonna' gallery in Milan.

1953 *February–March* He exhibits two groups of paintings on Calabrian subjects at the 'Il Pincio' gallery in Rome.

May–June The magazine *L'illustrazione italiana* publishes his article 'Contadini di Calabria' ('Peasants of Calabria').

1954 He takes part in the XXVIII Venice Biennale, exhibiting no fewer than 50 canvases in his own personal hall, with a catalogue introduction by Garosci.

He joins the group of neo-realist painters.

He writes prefaces to J. De Castro, *Geografia della fame* (originally published in Portuguese as *Geografia da fome*, 'Geography of Hunger'; Italian edition De Donato) and R. Scotellaro, *È fatto giorno* (Mondadori).

1955 *March* Solo exhibition with the series *Gli amanti* (*The Lovers*) at the 'Il Pincio' gallery in Rome, with a catalogue introduction by Calvino.

He takes part in the conference at Matera on Scotellaro.

He travels to the USSR and takes his third trip to Sicily.

He exhibits, at the VII Quadriennale of Rome, *Lamento per Rocco Scotellaro*.

He serves on a cabinet-level commission for the preservation of the Appian Way.

He publishes *Le parole sono pietre: Tre giornate in Sicilia* ('Words are Stones: Three Days in Sicily') with Einaudi.

He writes a preface to R. Scotellaro, *L'uva puttanella* (Laterza).

1956 *January* He travels to India.

3 December He publishes in *Il punto* a 'Lettera agli scrittori sovietici' ('Letter to Soviet Authors').

He publishes, with Einaudi, *Il futuro ha un cuore antico* ('The Future Has an Ancient Heart'), which later wins the Premio Viareggio.

1956–7 He publishes a series of essays on art criticism in *L'illustrazione italiana*.

1957 Commemoration of Di Vittorio, Dorso, and Salvemini.

17 November He delivers a speech on unemployment at the Teatro Politeama in Palermo.

He helps with the design of the headstone for Scotellaro.

He writes a preface to C. de Brosses, *Viaggio in Italia: Lettere familiari* (Italian edition of *Lettres familières d'Italie: Lettres écrites d'Italie en 1739 et 1740*), published with Parenti.

1958 *May* In the general election, he is a candidate for the Italian senate, as a member of the Partito Socialista Italiano ('Italian Socialist Party'), for the ward of Acireale.

He travels to Germany.

He writes a preface to L. Sterne, *La vita e le opinioni di Tristram Shandy, gentiluomo* (*The Life and Opinions of Tristram Shandy, Gentleman*), published with Einaudi.

1959 He travels to China. He publishes *La doppia notte dei tigli* (*The Two-Fold Night* or *The Linden Trees*) with Einaudi.

1960 *January* Group exhibition at the 'Chiurazzi' gallery in Rome. The seven canvases that he exhibits mark, according to critics, a watershed in Levi's artistic development.

May He delivers a speech on employment and development in southern Italy (a keynote address to the conference on work and development in southern Italy held in Palma di Montechiaro).

July Articles in *ABC* in the section 'Parole chiare' on the days of insurrection in Reggio Emilia.

6 August He delivers a speech at Reggio Emilia in the Piazza della Libertà on the thirtieth anniversary of the deaths of five anti-Fascists (it appears as a preface to R. Nicolai, *Reggio Emilia, 7 Luglio 1960*, Editori Riuniti).

He writes a preface to H. B. Stendhal, *Roma, Napoli e Firenze* (Italian edition of *Rome, Naples et Florence*), published with Parenti. He publishes *Un volto che ci somiglia: Ritratto dell'Italia* with Einaudi.

1961 *May* He executes a large oil panel painting, measuring 18.5 by 3.2 metres, for the Lucania Pavilion at the expo 'Italia' 61 – Mostra dell'Unità d'Italia' ('Italy' 61 – Exhibition of Italian Unity').

Preface to P. P. Pasolini, *Accattone* (F. M., Rome). He writes the preface to the catalogue of Guttuso's exhibition in Moscow.

1962 He signs the 'Appello dei 12', a document that demands that Italy have nothing to do with nuclear war.

April–May Solo exhibition at the 'La Nuova Pesa' gallery in Rome (works from 1929 to 1934), with a catalogue introduction by A. Del Guercio.

Second trip to Sardinia.

He writes a preface to *Autobiografia del fascismo*, edited by E. Nizza (La Pietra). He writes a preface to M. Pantaleone, *Mafia e politica* (Einaudi).

1963 Letters to Alicata and Khrushchev.

28 April He is elected senator in the ward of Civitavecchia as an independent running on the list of the Partito Comunista Italiano ('Italian Communist Party') and he joins the mixed group. He becomes a member of the Commissione Istruzione Pubblica e Belle Art ('Commission on Public Education and Fine Arts').

21 December First speech to the senate, on the Moro government.

Solo exhibition of drawings and monotypes at the 'La Cavourrina' gallery in Turin.

He writes a preface to I. Buttitta, *La peddi nova* (Feltrinelli). He writes a preface to *Notte sull'Europa*, edited by F. Etnasi and R. Forti (Rome).

1964 He becomes a member of the commission of enquiry for the protection and exploitation of historic, archaeological, artistic, and natural resources (Franceschini Commission). He oversees with the Honourable Vedovato the second study group, charged with investigating medieval, modern, and contemporary historic and artistic resources, and develops the report on contemporary art (published in the first volume of the *Atti della commissione* ('Proceedings of the Commission'), p. 381).

14 April Speech to the senate on cultural resources.

1 August Speech to the senate on the vote of confidence in the second Moro government.

He publishes *Tutto il miele è finito* ('All the Honey is Gone') with Einaudi.

1965 He participates in numerous exhibitions commemorating the Resistance.

Between September and October, he exhibits 48 works in the historic retrospective 'I Sei di Torino', organized by the Galleria Civica d'Arte Moderna ('City Gallery of Modern Art') in Turin.

1966 *26 October* Speech to the senate on speculation in housing at Agrigento.

11 November Speech to the Italian senate on the Florence flood.

Solo exhibition at the 'Piemonte Artistico e Culturale' gallery in Turin. He exhibits 90 landscape paintings of Alassio.

He writes a preface to the catalogue of Guttuso's exhibition in East Berlin.

1967 *May* Solo exhibition at the Circolo Culturale 'Rinascita' in Matera. He exhibits 71 works, from 1935 to 1967, of southern Italian subjects.

27 June Speech to the senate on the law governing the police.

June Solo exhibition at the 'Pro-Loco' in Nereto (Teramo province).

He founds, with P. Cinanni and others, the Federazione Italiana Lavoratori Emigrati e Famiglie ('Italian Federation of Emigrant Workers and Their Families').

A special supplement of the magazine *Galleria* is published (XVII, 3–6, May–December), dedicated to Carlo Levi, with numerous essays and reminiscences. The supplement also includes previously unpublished writings.

He writes a preface to U. Saba, *L'amicizia* (Mondadori).

1968 Solo exhibition at the 'La Nuova Pesa' gallery in Rome.

19 May He is re-elected to the senate from the ward of Velletri on the list of the Partito Comunista Italiano-Partito Socialista di Unità Proletaria ('Italian Communist Party-Italian Socialist Party of Proletarian Unity'). He forms part of the parliamentary group of the independent left. He becomes a member of the commission on foreign affairs.

1969 *May* Solo exhibitions at the 'La Barcaccia' gallery in Rome (where he was to exhibit his work often in the years that follow) and in Montecatini.

11 August Speech to the senate on the crisis of the centre-left.

1970 *7 April* Speech to the senate on the Rumor government.

September In the context of the second edition of *Incontri Silani*, an extensive retrospective exhibition is organized by M. De Micheli at Lorica (Sila) with works relating to southern Italy.

1971 *January* Retrospective exhibition at the 'La Gradiva' gallery in Florence.

October Solo exhibition at the 'La Noce' gallery in Rome, featuring graphic works.

1973 *28 January* He suffers a detached retina, and undergoes two operations at the San Domenico hospital of Rome. He executes, in a temporary state of blindness, 140 drawings, and writes, with the help of a special easel, a text that will be published, after his death, as *Quaderno a cancelli* (Einaudi).

1974 *March* He is commissioned, along with Cagli and Guttuso, by General Beolchini to execute three artworks in commemoration of the massacre of the Ardeatine Caves. Cagli illustrates the oppression, Guttuso the massacre, and Levi the liberation. The artworks are then donated to the monumental complex on 25 March.

September Solo exhibition at the Palazzo Te in Mantua. This is the first great retrospective exhibition, with some 200 works, from 1922 to 1974, and it enjoys great interest and attention from critics and the public. At the conclusion of the show, a round table is held with the participation of U. Attardi, Pasolini, Soldati, and Del Guercio on the topic of 'Literary Influences and Civil Engagement in the Pictorial Career of C. Levi'.

December Between the 7th and the 10th of the month he makes his last visit to Basilicata (Lucania), presenting a portfolio of seven lithographic prints inspired by *Cristo si è fermato a Eboli*, published by Editore Esposito of Turin.

23 December He is admitted to hospital at the Policlinico Umberto I, in Rome.

He writes a preface to R. Scotellaro, *Uno si distrae al bivio* (Laterza). Preface to P. Cinanni, *Emigrazione e unità operaria* (Feltrinelli).

1975 *4 January* He dies after several days in a coma. He is buried in Aliano. The 'Persiana' gallery in Palermo exhibits his last work, *Apollo e Dafne* (*Apollo and Daphne*), executed on a goatskin drum the day before he is admitted to hospital.

Coraggio dei miti: Scritti contemporanei 1922–1974 ('The Courage of the Meek: Contemporary Writings 1922–1974') an anthology of writings, some unpublished, is published posthumously, edited by G. De Donato.

Index